Spitfire

A Photographic Biography

Dilip Sarkar

AMBERLEY

Sadly, not only servicemen and women, and their families, suffer in time of war. On 24 September 1940, Supermarine's Spitfire factory at Woolston in Southampton was successfully attacked by *Erprobungsgruppe* 210's fighter-bombers. The two youngest casualties beside the River Itchen that day were Douglas Cruickshank, a workshop assistant, aged fourteen, and nineteen-year-old Margaret Anne Moon, a typist. It is to those two teenagers that this book is respectfully dedicated.

First published 2013

Amberley Publishing
The Hill, Stroud
Gloucestershire, GL5 4EP

www.amberley-books.com

Copyright © Dilip Sarkar, 2013

The right of Dilip Sarkar to be identified as the Author of this work has been asserted in accordance with the Copyrights, Designs and Patents Act 1988.

ISBN 978 1 4456 0585 2

British Library Cataloguing in Publication Data.
A catalogue record for this book is available from the British Library.

Typeset in 11pt on 12pt Sabon LT Std.
Typesetting by Amberley Publishing.
Printed in the UK.

CONTENTS

PREFACE

The Supermarine Spitfire is the most charismatic and inspirational fighter aircraft ever built. Fascination for it certainly shows no sign of abating. In this book, therefore, I have tried to put the Spitfire into its design and operational context – mainly through the use of original photographs. Whereas my previous works have concentrated on the human experience connected with the Spitfire, this book focuses on the aircraft itself. The photographs are from a variety of sources, mainly from the personal collections of pilots and support staff. Although not of a professional photographer's standard, these nonetheless provide a unique window through which we can still glimpse the past – and are often much more interesting and revealing than the officially sanctioned images so widely available today. Sadly, most of the contributors are now deceased, but I remain grateful to all for their friendship and co-operation. The Spitfire's 'Finest Hour' was, of course, during the early war years, so I make no apology for having allocated more photographs to the years 1936–41.

I would also like to thank Roger Henderson, Henry Fargus, Steve Bown and Garry Campion for adding several extra illustrations, and my publisher, Jonathan Reeve, for suggesting this book. Indeed, I look forward to publication of Roger's book, The Channel Front: A Chronicle of 19 Squadron at War, 1941–42. Rob Rooker's boundless enthusiasm for all things related to 152 'Hyderabad' Squadron led to him founding and maintaining what is undoubtedly the best squadron-based website available: see http://www.152hyderabad.co.uk. Rob has also collected numerous photographs from veterans, and I am particularly grateful to him for contributing a number of them to this project.

My wife, Karen, of course, has my love and gratitude for her continued, unfailing, and essential support.

Dilip Sarkar MBE FRHistS BA(Hons),
Worcester, 26 April 2013

1

'A REAL KILLER FIGHTER': 1936–1939

In the psyche of the British public, R. J. Mitchell's Supermarine Spitfire was a winner from the outset. This was not just because of its stunning sleek lines, elliptical wing and high performance, but because the Spitfire was a direct descendant from Mitchell's famous Schneider Trophy-winning British seaplane racers. This spectacular competition took place between 1919 and 1931, aircraft racing at low level over water, providing a breathtaking spectacle for spectators. The matter became one of great national pride. Aircraft designers began pushing the boundaries, breaking away from the traditional biplane and producing faster and more streamlined monoplanes. Mitchell, the chief designer of Supermarine at Southampton, was at the forefront of this development. In 1927, Mitchell's S5 achieved first and second place, setting a new air speed record of 281.66 mph. In 1929, the improved S6 won again, with an average speed of 328.63 mph. Afterwards, the S6 was confirmed as the fastest and most technologically advanced aircraft in the world when Squadron Leader Orlebar set a new world record at 357.7 mph. Britain needed one more consecutive victory to permanently retain the coveted silver trophy but the dreadful Wall Street Crash dictated the withdrawal of government funding for the next race. An eccentric patriot, Lady Houston, incensed at the prospect of Britain being unable to compete, then wrote a cheque for £100,000 – enabling Mitchell to win the Schneider Trophy in 1931 with the S6B's staggering 340.08 mph. In spite of the seaplane's high performance and the patriotic fervour generated by the race, the RAF's Air Member for Supply & Research, Air Vice-Marshal Hugh Dowding, considered the racing seaplanes useless for military purposes. Nonetheless, Dowding had recognised the clear superiority of monoplanes, leading to the issue of Specification F7/30 on 1 October 1931, which invited private tenders from aircraft designers to produce a new fighter for the RAF. As Dowding said, 'I wanted to … cash in on the experience gained in aircraft construction and engine progress.' The Spitfire story had begun.

The requirements for F7/30 were:

1. Highest possible rate of climb.
2. Highest possible speed at 15,000 feet.
3. Fighting view.
4. Manoeuvrability.
5. Capability of ease and rapid production in quantity.
6. Ease of maintenance.

The Air Ministry also required the new fighter's maximum speed to be at least 250 mph, and for it to carry four machine-guns. Surprisingly, Gloster Aircraft won the competition with a radial-engined biplane, the SS37, although this never entered production. Fortunately the Air Ministry recognised that the design's edge in performance was insufficient, meaning that it would soon become obsolete. Mitchell had found F7/30 'too restrictive … to produce an aircraft of the highest possible performance'. Consequently Supermarine and aero-manufacturer Rolls-Royce decided to privately collaborate on a 'real killer fighter'. The Air Ministry was notified of this and advised that under no circumstances would any official interference be tolerated. In November 1934, therefore, Mitchell began work on his 'Type 300 Fighter'.

A month later, the Air Ministry commissioned Supermarine to produce an 'improved F7/30 design', from which point the project became government funded. On 3 January 1935, Supermarine confirmed this arrangement and provided details of their new machine. This specification included all the F7/30 requirements in addition to a tail wheel, as opposed to the more traditional skid, and wing-mounted machine-guns firing beyond the propeller arc. While this work was in progress, in April 1935 the Air Ministry redefined its requirement for the new 'Single-Engine Single-Seater Day and Night Fighter' in F10/35. The main points were:

1. Had to be at least 40 mph faster than contemporary bombers at 15,000 feet.
2. 'Have a number of forward firing machine-guns that can produce the maximum hitting power possible in the shortest space of time available for one attack.' The Air Ministry 'considered that eight guns should be provided'.
3. Had to achieve 'the maximum possible and not less than 310 mph at 15,000 feet at maximum power with the highest speed possible between 5,000 and 15,000 feet'.
4. Have the best possible climbing performance to 20,000 feet, although this was considered of secondary importance to 'speed and hitting power'.
5. Be armed with at least six but preferably eight machine-guns, all forward firing and wing-mounted outside the propeller arc. These were to be fired by 'electrical means'. In the event of six guns being used, 400 rounds per gun was necessary, 300 if eight were fitted.
6. Had to be 'a steady firing platform'.
7. Had to include the following 'special features' and equipment:
a) Enclosed cockpit.
b) Cockpit heating.
c) Night flying equipment.
d) Radio Telephony (R/T).
e) Oxygen for two-and-a-half hours.
f) Easily accessed and maintained guns.
g) Retractable undercarriage and tail wheel.
h) Wheel brakes.

Such an aircraft would indeed be a 'real killer fighter'. Interestingly, however, the Air Staff did not dictate that it must be a monoplane, indicating that monoplanes were not yet considered supreme in the corridors of Whitehall.

The requirement for eight machine-guns was significant. A study in 1932 concluded that more guns were required to destroy a modern bomber. It was believed that the new breed of monoplane fighters would be so fast as to permit their pilots just one pass: the more guns brought to bear, therefore, for those few seconds the better. The choice of the .303 rifle-calibre Browning gun would prove a mistake, however. Bitter experience in the early stages of the Second World War indicated that a heavier projectile was much better, and preferably a cannon shell. Nevertheless, the new specification and thought process reflected progress.

In 1933, Adolf Hitler and the Nazis came to power in Germany, the clouds of war quickening over Europe thereafter. The following year, the RAF's annual air exercise was a fiasco, only two of the five bombers engaged in a mock attack being intercepted. Incredibly, Britain's air defences at the time were incapable of dealing with more than five raiders simultaneously. Indeed, the prevalent air doctrine of the day was entirely focussed upon the bomber delivering a knock-out blow, meaning that the emphasis of production and development was focussed upon the bomber force. The year before Hitler became Chancellor, in fact, the British Prime Minister Stanley Baldwin told the House of Commons that 'the bomber would always get through' and that 'the only defence is offence, meaning that you have to kill more women and children more quickly than the enemy if you want to save yourselves'. Air Chief Marshal Sir Hugh Trenchard, the 'Father of the RAF', agreed, stating in 1921 that the aeroplane 'was a shockingly bad weapon for defence', and that the use of fighters was justified only 'to keep up the morale of your own people'. Defence spending, therefore, was effectively sidelined and provided only the bare minimum of resources. So little was spent on re-armament, in fact, that Winston Churchill described the years 1931–35 as those of 'the locust'. By 1935, though, it was clear that although Germany was unlikely to be ready for war until 1939, Hitler's preparations were so advanced that the threat could no longer be ignored. Consequently, at last, Britain began to re-arm. In August 1936, German forces were deployed to Spain, fighting on behalf of the fascist General Franco, providing Hitler with an opportunity to test new weapons and tactics. On 27 April 1936, German bombers caused great damage to and loss of civilian life at Guernica – emphasising to many Baldwin's ominous prediction. Others, including Dowding – fortunately soon to play a key role in the air defence of Britain – disagreed, believing that the fighter was an essential weapon. Challenging Trenchard's policy, Dowding argued that unless the home base could be adequately protected against enemy bombers, it would be impossible for the bomber force to deliver a knock-out or counter blow against the enemy. Ultimately events would prove him right; but it was clear now that, in any case, the RAF desperately needed its new 'killer fighter'.

Mitchell's first design, the Type 224, was unsuccessful, however, which is actually why the Hawker Hurricane fighter, designed by Sydney Camm, flew before the Spitfire and became available in large numbers quicker than the Spitfire. Mitchell knew, in fact, that time was running out on two counts: firstly, and obviously, the threat from Nazi Germany, and secondly because, having been diagnosed with rectal cancer, he was dying. Not knowing whether fate would provide him sufficient time to complete the project, Mitchell continued working on the Type 300. The result – the Supermarine Spitfire, so called after the Supermarine chairman's nickname for his daughter – was immediately striking, akin to a winged bullet, elliptical wings providing a unique signature. The prototype, K5054, first flew from Southampton's Eastleigh airfield on 5 March 1936. This twenty-minute test flight was entirely successful. On 3 June 1936 the Air Ministry ordered 310 Spitfires at a cost of £4,500 each (excluding engine, guns, instruments and radios). It was expected that the first Spitfires would be delivered to the RAF in October 1937, but it soon became apparent that Supermarine – a small company of only 500 employees – lacked the capacity to fulfil large orders. Eventually, the first Spitfire was delivered on 19 July 1938. Tragically, Mitchell himself had not lived to see the moment: this brilliant aircraft designer died, aged forty-two, on 11 June 1937. On 4 August 1938, Supermarine Test Pilot Jeffrey Quill delivered the first operational aircraft, K9789, to 19 Squadron at Duxford, which was equipped with obsolete Gloster Gauntlet biplanes at that time. Flight Sergeant George Unwin took one look at the new monoplane and decided that 'this was the fighter I wanted to go to war with. It was a decision I never had occasion to regret.'

Hawker's Hurricane fighter had first flown on 6 November 1935, 111 Squadron receiving the first production Hurricane in November 1937. It has often been argued that because Camm's design relied upon traditional construction techniques, as opposed to the all metal, monocoque construction of the Spitfire, it was easier to produce and henceforth why the Air Ministry initially ordered more Hurricanes than Spitfires. That may to some extent be so, but the Hurricane's lack of a metal-covered wing was a design deficiency, taking some time to rectify. This is an early indication that the Hurricane was inferior not only to the Spitfire but – much more ominously – Germany's Me 109. Professor Willy Messerschmitt's 'Augsburg Eagle' was the first of the three fighters to fly, in May 1935.

The new German monoplane fighter had been designed around the concept of the smallest, and therefore lightest, airframe around the most powerful engine. This featured a metal-alloy framework, flush-riveted stressed metal covering, leading-edge wing slots in conjunction with slotted trailing-edge flaps, which increased the wing area upon demand, retractable undercarriage and a jettisonable canopy. The 109 was initially armed with two nose-mounted 7.92 mm machine-guns, and, like the original Hurricanes and Spitfires, a wooden fixed-pitch propeller. Blooded during the Spanish Civil War, the 109 set a new world speed record of 379.38 mph. This unprecedented speed was achieved because of the aircraft's new Daimler-Benz 601 engine. Spitfires and Hurricanes were both powered by the Rolls-Royce Merlin engine, the Mk III variant of which, during the Battle of Britain ahead, being more powerful than the DB601A at all altitudes. The German engine, however, had one great advantage: it was fuel injected and therefore unaffected by gravity, negative G causing the Merlin's float-type carburettor to cut out momentarily in the dive, meaning that the 109 could always outpace a Spitfire in that attitude. The 109's fixed-pitch propeller was soon replaced by the three-bladed VDM 'controllable pitch' airscrew, permitting rotation of the blades through 360°, enabling the selection of the optimum setting for any situation. The British fighters were first updated to the De Havilland two-pitch propeller – fine pitch for take-off, coarse for flight. Although the British were developing their Constant Speed (CS) propeller, which was comparable to the VDM unit, this would not be fitted to all RAF fighters until 16 August 1940 – during the Battle of Britain itself – increasing the Spitfire's rate of climb by 730 feet per minute.

In respect of fighter armament, the Germans initially lagged behind the British. News that the new RAF fighters were armed with eight machine-guns led to a rapid re-think. The difficulty was that the 109's wings were so thin that it could not carry more than two guns. The effect of a further pair of machine-guns was really inconsequential, so it was decided to wing-mount two 20 mm MG-FF Oerlikon cannons. This weapon's muzzle velocity was much lower than a machine-gun: eight rounds per second to the machine-gun's seventeen. Regardless, there was no comparison between the destructive power of a puny machine-gun bullet and a fist-sized cannon shell – just one strike from such a round could prove fatal. Machine-guns, though, provide a spread effect, much like a shotgun, and are therefore more suited to the average shot, rather than the exceptional marksman; this combination of both machine-gun and cannon gave the Germans the best of both worlds. Although a circumstance arrived at more by accident than intention, this too would prove immeasurably advantageous in the early battles ahead.

After the Munich Crisis of 1938, Hitler became increasingly confident and became focussed upon an aggressive expansionist policy. Even so, many believed that Hitler was merely rectifying what were seen as various injustices imposed upon Germany by the Versailles Peace Treaty of 1919, but the violent events of 1 September 1939 indicated the Führer's true intentions: Germany invaded Poland. Hitler ignored an ultimatum from Britain and France to withdraw his troops immediately, and so, with a heavy hart, the British Prime Minister, Neville Chamberlain – who had personally worked indefatigably to appease the Nazi dictator and avoid another world war – broadcast to the British people on 3 September 1939 that the country was at war with Nazi Germany. The time had come for Supermarine's 'real killer fighter' to prove its worth in anger.

In 1936, RAF Fighter Command had been created with responsibility for the air defence of Britain. The country was divided into four fighter groups and the British Isles were surrounded by an invisible ring of radar beams, providing early warning of an enemy air attack. The chief and creator of this System of Air Defence was none other than the former Air Member for Supply & Development, now Air Chief Marshal Sir Hugh Dowding. At the outbreak of war, however, the fighter scenario was not entirely optimistic. Fighter Command possessed sixteen squadrons of Hurricanes – some 497 aircraft – eleven of which remained at home, while four went to France with the Advance Air Striking Force. Only 187 Spitfires were operational, just eleven squadrons in total, all of which were retained for home defence. It is often argued that the opposing air forces were numerically equally matched, which may be so, but some stark statistics require consideration to correctly appreciate the situation Dowding faced. In addition to their Spitfires and Hurricanes, Fighter Command also had fifteen other fighter squadrons. The fact is, though, that eight of these were flying obsolete Gloster Gladiator biplanes, and seven the twin-engined Bristol Blenheim Mk IF. The latter would ultimately prove useless as a day fighter, as did its enemy counterpart the Me 110, and be relegated to night fighting. It was only, therefore, the twenty-seven Hurricanes and Spitfires that mattered so far as a daylight contest was concerned. Against this force were ranged 850 operational Me 109s (supplemented by 195 Me 110s).

Before war came in 1939, Fighter Command had no point of reference so far as devising tactics for the new monoplane fighters was concerned. There were several factors to consider. Firstly, and significantly, it was wrongly believed that due to the high speeds achieved by this new generation of fighters, fighter-to-fighter combat, like in the First World War, would be impossible. The human body, they thought, would simply be unable to cope with the high levels of negative G and other physical strains imposed by high speed manoeuvres. Moreover, the range of fighters, being short-range defensive machines, is limited (Spitfire Mk I: 395 miles, Hawker Hurricane Mk I: 505 miles, Me 109E: 412 miles). Given the distance between Britain and Germany, any intrusion over British air space was expected to be by longer-range bombers, and, indeed, small formations of them. Twin-engined bombers, being slower and less manoeuvrable than single-engined fighters, were considered easy to shoot down – especially if the RAF fighters were closely bunched together and operating in concert, so as to simultaneously bring multiple guns to bear. The standard Fighter Command formation became the 'vic' of three aircraft, the squadron of twelve being sub-divided into such sections. Each section could attack with twenty-four guns in a single pass – against an enemy bomber which was expected to obligingly continue straight and level, taking little or no evasive action. Each section would attack successively, raking the target with a total of ninety-six machine-guns. The involvement of enemy fighters was not a consideration in this scenario, their limited range restricting their activities to defending their own nation's air space – not engaging in long-range offensive operations.

Certainly the experience of RAF pilots during 1939 and early 1940 gave no indication of how wrong the Fighter Command tacticians would ultimately be proved in due course. Although the anticipated and immediate attempt at a 'knock-out blow' by the Luftwaffe failed to materialise, it was indeed only German bombers that were active over England. On 16 October 1939, the first air attack on Britain took place when thirty Ju 88s of I/KG 30 attacked British shipping in the Firth of Forth. At 3.30 p.m., Flight Lieutenant George Pinkerton of 602 Squadron scored the Spitfire's first aerial victory by shooting down one of these raiders which crashed into the sea off Port Seton. Such enemy raids continued, as did Spitfire successes against them. On 21 October the Hurricane recorded its first combat successes, when three mine-laying He 115 seaplanes were shot down off Yorkshire by 46 Squadron. Enemy bombers were also destroyed over France by Hurricanes – and so, for the first few months following the outbreak of war, what Flight Lieutenant Brian Lane described as a 'queer war' continued, with still no sign of the dreaded 'knock-out' blow. Again ominously, however, the Air Ministry concluded that 'there is no doubt that by 1939 the Me 109 was superior to any Allied fighter except the Spitfire, which, however, was then only available to the RAF in small numbers'. Fortunately in the months that followed, British aircraft production began exceeding German output, and as Spitfire production stepped up, via a system of sub-contracting, more of Mitchell's 'real killer fighter' reached the squadrons – but would it be enough?

1. The brilliant British aircraft designer R. J. Mitchell, chief designer at Supermarine. His advanced thinking regarding the superiority of monoplanes led to the Spitfire. Sadly, Mitchell died prematurely, aged forty-two, on 11 June 1937 – his work on a heavy bomber design unfinished.

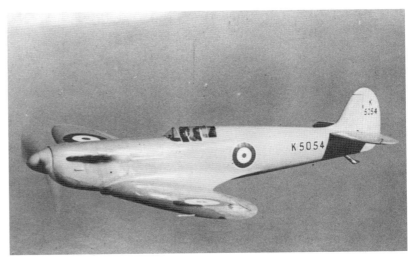

Below: 2. Mitchell's Schneider Trophy-winning S6 seaplane racer. The sleek lines are clearly apparent.

Right: 3. The prototype Spitfire, K5054.

Below right: 4. The only known photograph of R. J. Mitchell with his Spitfire, photographed at Eastleigh by his son, Gordon.

Spitfire

Left: 5. Naturally Supermarine fanfared their new fighter. This is the cover of the original promotional catalogue, *c. 1938*.

Below left: 6. The Supermarine factory before the war, situated on the banks of the River Itchen at Southampton. The site no longer exists, having been cleared in more recent times to make way for the Itchen Bridge.

Below: 7. Another Spitfire prototype, resplendent in war paint.

Above: 8. Supermarine Test Pilot Jeffrey Quill over Southampton at the controls of the same aircraft.

Right: 9. Early Spitfire fuselages under construction at Supermarine.

Above left: 10. Another pre-war advertisement featuring the Spitfire – this time by Rolls-Royce, the aero engines of which powered the Supermarine 'Real Killer Fighter'.

Below left: 11. More early Spitfires being built at Supermarine.

Left: 12. An early Supermarine advertisement promoting the Spitfire.

Above: 13. A pre-war Wills Cigarette card featuring the Spitfire.

Above right: 14. A close-up of a 19 Squadron Spitfire Mk I.

Right: 15. The Spitfire was first delivered to Duxford's 19 Squadron on 4 August 1938. Here, the Squadron's Spitfire Mk Is are lined up for the press in 1939. Note the fixed-pitch propeller, lack of armoured glass, un-faired radio mast, and pre-war 'WZ' codes.

Above: 16. Spitfire Mk IAs of 66 and 19 Squadrons at Duxford in 1939.

Left: 17. A close-up indicating the thin wing-section and Browning machine-gun ports.

Opposite: 18. Given developments in Germany, the Spitfire was soon fitted with the De Havilland two-pitch, three-bladed airscrew. This machine, having its markings applied at Eastleigh before a production test flight, is one of those aircraft, designated Mk IA. By now the Spitfire's windscreen was armoured, the sliding canopy blown, improving visibility, and the radio mast faired.

Left: 19. Flight Lieutenant Brian Lane leading 19 Squadron's 'A' Flight over Cambridgeshire in early 1940. This rare air-to-air snapshot was taken by Pilot Officer Michael Lane.

Below: 20. 19 Squadron's first Spitfire flying accident. Two aircraft, K9854, flown by Pilot Officer Eric Ball, and this, K9821, flown by Flying Officer Wilf Clouston, collided in mid-air. Clouston forced-landed on Newmarket race course – fortunately both pilots were unhurt.

Opposite: 21. Another cutaway drawing, this time from *Flight* magazine, showing an early Spitfire.

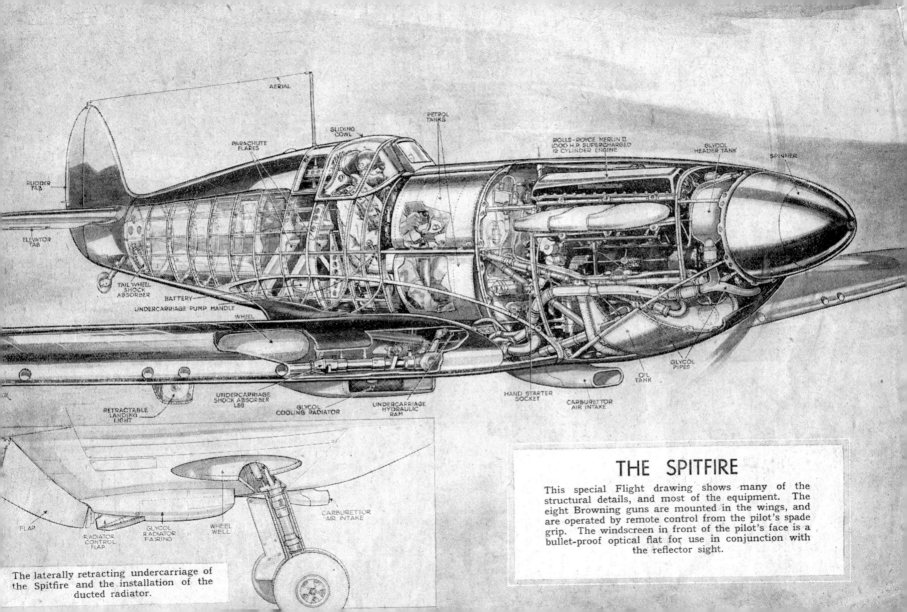

AERIAL

PARACHUTE FLARES

SLIDING COWL

PETROL TANKS

ROLLS-ROYCE MERLIN II
1,000 H.P. SUPERCHARGED
12 CYLINDER ENGINE

GLYCOL HEADER TANK

SPINNER

RUDDER TAB

ELEVATOR TAB

TAIL WHEEL SHOCK ABSORBER

BATTERY

UNDERCARRIAGE PUMP HANDLE

WHEEL

RETRACTABLE LANDING LIGHT

UNDERCARRIAGE SHOCK ABSORBER LEG

GLYCOL COOLING RADIATOR

UNDERCARRIAGE HYDRAULIC RAM

HAND STARTER SOCKET

CARBURETTOR AIR INTAKE

OIL TANK

GLYCOL PIPES

FLAP

RADIATOR CONTROL FLAP

GLYCOL RADIATOR FAIRING

WHEEL WELL

CARBURETTOR AIR INTAKE

THE SPITFIRE

This special Flight drawing shows many of the structural details, and most of the equipment. The eight Browning guns are mounted in the wings, and are operated by remote control from the pilot's spade grip. The windscreen in front of the pilot's face is a bullet-proof optical flat for use in conjunction with the reflector sight.

The laterally retracting undercarriage of the Spitfire and the installation of the ducted radiator.

2

SPITFIRE SUPREME: 1940

On 26 March 1940 the RAF destroyed its first Me 109. This was not achieved by a Spitfire, however, and, Spitfire squadrons being based entirely at home, it was only the Hurricanes in France that had such an opportunity. On that day, 73 Squadron engaged enemy fighters over Saarlautern and Trier, claiming four destroyed and two unconfirmed. On 9 April 1940 the 'Phoney War' ended abruptly when Germany invaded Norway. Although a British task force was rapidly despatched, the Royal Navy (RN) failed to prevent a successful enemy seaborne landing. Naturally this increased Dowding's concern for the defence of Britain, and emphasised the importance of preserving his small fighter force for home defence. On 2 May 1940 a comparison took place between a captured Me 109 and a Hurricane. The 109 was found to be up to 40 mph faster but unable to out-turn the Hawker fighter. It was also evident that unless the Hurricane was rapidly fitted with a CS propeller, it would continue to be at a significant height disadvantage. The superiority of Luftwaffe fighter tactics was also evident. These had been worked out in Spain, and relied upon three things: height, sun and a tactical formation known as the *schwarm*. Unlike their RAF counterparts, the Germans had actual combat experience with the Me 109, and realised very quickly that aircraft should be spread out, unlike the RAF 'vic'. Maintaining a respectable distance between aircraft of around 200 metres, the enemy pilots did not have to concentrate on formation flying, but could instead search for the enemy. Further, the German fighters flew in a line abreast formation and in a section of four, the aircraft occupying the positions of an outstretched hand's fingertips. The foremost aircraft was the section leader. The extreme left aircraft was the leader's wingman, the position being reversed for the right-hand pair. In combat the *schwarm* broke into these two fighting pairs, the leader's job being to attack, covered by his wingman. Another crucial factor was the 109's superior service ceiling (36,000 feet) compared to the Hurricane and Spitfire Mk I (34,000 feet). Height, enabling a fighter leader to position himself between the enemy and the dazzling sun, achieved surprise: and surprise was everything.

On 10 May 1940 Hitler attacked the West, German forces invading Belgium, Holland, Luxembourg and France. Airborne troops and motorised infantry, supported by tanks and aircraft operating as flying artillery, isolated, enveloped and paralysed the Allies. The tragedy of the Fall of France has often been told, so it is unnecessary to re-visit that narrative here. The crucial thing for our purposes is that Dowding refused to send Spitfires to France and waste them on a battle already lost, this being further evidence of the Spitfire's superiority. The catastrophic events in France, however, coupled with the total absence of any attempt by the German bombers to administer a 'knock-out' blow on Britain, were throwing British air power experts into confusion. Over the battlefields of France the Me 109 achieved complete aerial superiority, enabling German ground forces to operate unhindered by RAF air attacks. John Terraine has rightly argued that a strong and appropriately equipped Allied fighter force was the only thing capable of preventing this. The Germans had given the Allies a devastating lesson in the benefit of possessing and correctly deploying a modern fighter force. From this point onwards it was clear that the bomber-orientated air doctrine of the inter-war period was completely flawed. In a nutshell, Trenchard was wrong and Dowding, thankfully as future events would further prove, was right. Suddenly the fighter aircraft achieved a level of usefulness and potency hitherto unconsidered by the British.

By 26 May 1940, the British Expeditionary Force (BEF) had no alternative but to retire on and be evacuated from the Channel port of Dunkirk. The story of this operation, codenamed DYNAMO, is well known and has a special place in the British popular memory of the Second World War. The fact remains, however, that the BEF had suffered high casualties and left behind all armour and heavy equipment. Although the British propaganda machine hailed Dunkirk as a victory, and there can be no doubt that the rescue of 340,000 troops was a welcome deliverance, it is as well to remember that wars are not won by evacuations. It was during the appended protective air operation that the Spitfire met the Me 109 for the first time. Until

now, Dowding had preserved his precious Spitfires for home defence, but so hard pressed had the Hurricane squadrons been in France that he was now forced to commit Spitfires to the battle raging across the Channel. There was a high risk factor involved, given that Dunkirk lay 50 miles across the sea from 11 Group's closest airfields; this meant two sea crossings per patrol and, of course, any contact was likely to be over the French coast. Spitfires shot down were likely, therefore, to crash into the sea or perhaps crash-land in France, resulting in the capture of pilots. Those who bailed out into the sea faced the prospect of rescue with uncertainty, given that formal air-sea rescue arrangements were woefully inadequate or non-existent. The operation was placed in the capable hands of Air Vice-Marshal Keith Park, commander of 11 Group. The Spitfire force available amounted to just sixteen squadrons, meaning that the provision of a constant fighter umbrella over the Dunkirk beaches during daylight was impossible. All Fighter Command could do was its best under difficult circumstances. Ironically, therefore, the Spitfire's first real test came not as a short-range defensive interceptor, but an offensive fighter operating at a range well beyond that envisaged by Mitchell. Fortunately at this time, Fighter Command's pilots were given one performance advantage: 100 octane fuel, significantly improving the Merlin's boost and aircraft's rate of climb. Emergency boost, of +12lbs per square inch could be used in an emergency, to get a pilot either quickly to action or out of trouble, but only for a few minutes. Spitfire pilots fighting over Dunkirk would often be thankful for this expedient.

The first big air battle between the opposing fighter forces took place over Calais on 23 May. The Spitfires of 54 Squadron claimed three 109s destroyed, 92 Squadron two. The balance sheet at close of play was unfavourable to Fighter Command, however: seven Spitfires had been destroyed and ten pilots lost in total. As the operation continued, the air fighting increased and intensified. On 26 May, 19 Squadron was particularly roughly handled by 109s while attacking a formation of slow Stukas over Calais. The Commanding Officer (CO), Squadron Leader Geoffrey Stephenson, led his four vics of three, throttled right back to match the dive-bombers' speed, in a textbook Fighter Command attack. High above, hidden by the sun, Me 109 pilots must have watched this scene below with utter disbelief. It took just seconds for the enemy fighters to crash through 19 Squadron, breaking up the ridiculously precise and impractical formations, and shooting down two Spitfires: Stephenson subsequently crash-landed on the beach, spending the remainder of the war as a prisoner; Pilot Officer Watson was never seen again.

The battle was far from one-sided though. As the days wore on Park began operating his squadrons in multiples of four, although, largely due to communication difficulties and because such a scenario was unpredicted, these did not operate as a 'wing', in the way that comparable formations did from 1941 onwards. It was more a case of squadrons travelling across the sea in convoy, arriving over the French coast together and in numbers. Once battle was joined, though, the formations completely lost cohesion. As the Spitfire pilots gained in experience daily, the Germans soon developed a grudging respect for the Spitfire, described in the *Luftwaffe War Diaries* as possessing a comparable performance to the Me 109E. Indeed, over the French coast at least, the balance of power shifted completely in the Spitfire pilots' favour – and for the purposes of the evacuation below, that was where it mattered at that desperate time. Certainly Park considered that his force had achieved 'total ascendency' over the German bombers, and that 'the Spitfire performed very well at Dunkirk'. Moreover, the deficiencies highlighted in RAF tactical

doctrine, techniques and procedures could be improved in time for the coming Battle of Britain.

On the night of 18/19 June 1940, the Spitfire recorded its first nocturnal victory. Neither the Hurricane or Spitfire were created as night fighters, and the Spitfire in particular, due to its narrow-track undercarriage, was never a great night flyer. Nonetheless, so unprepared were Britain's night-time defences that the experiment to use both types after dark was justified. At 12.30 a.m. that night, Flight Lieutenant A. G. 'Sailor' Malan of 74 Squadron destroyed a He 111 near Chelmsford, followed by another forty-five minutes later. Such successes, however, proved rare. France formally surrendered on 22 June 1940. There followed a short lull, as both sides retired to take stock. On 27 June, experimental cannon-armed Spitfires were delivered to 19 Squadron at Fowlmere in the Duxford Sector of 12 Group. The fighting over France had highlighted the advantages of the 109's 20 mm cannon, an omission Fighter Command needed to swiftly address. The Me 109's wing section was extremely thin, but German engineers had accommodated the Oerlikon's ammunition drum by fitting blisters to the upper and under wing surfaces. Surprisingly, given that captured 109s had been examined, this the Air Ministry did not do. The 20 mm Hispano Suiza cannon was side-mounted, so as to be accommodated by the Spitfire's wing section. Shells were belt-fed from boxes, instead of the intended drum, but in combat, as the wing flexed, stoppages occurred as shell cases jammed upon ejection. This Spitfire, the Mk IB, was only armed with two cannon, so if one or both weapons jammed the pilot was not only obliged to break off any action but was extremely vulnerable. During most of the summer ahead, this problem would continue to vex 19 Squadron, as a solution was sought. Some squadrons previously engaged over Dunkirk also recognised the impracticality of Fighter Command's stipulated tactics, and so began many ad hoc experiments by certain squadron commanders to devise their own preferred formations.

The occupation of France by the enemy changed everything, so far as the defence of Britain was concerned. The vital importance of aerial superiority over the battlefield had been demonstrated to shocking effect by the Luftwaffe fighters over France. Operating from bases in Northern France, even London was now within range of the Me 109. Although the 109's limited fuel capacity provided only twenty minutes flying time over the British capital, this meant that London was at great risk of daylight attack by German bombers. Far from being alone or in small groups, as the Fighter Command tacticians originally expected, the enemy bombers could now be escorted by large numbers of Me 109s – all the way to London and back. As Winston Churchill, who had replaced Chamberlain as Prime Minister on 10 May, told the nation, 'The Battle of France is over. I expect that the Battle of Britain is about to begin.'

The Battle of Britain's bibliography is enormous, and it is not my intention to provide a narrative here. Instead I would refer readers to my book *The Few: The Battle of Britain in the Words of the Pilots* (Amberley, 2009). It is necessary, though, to appreciate some key points. Firstly the Battle of Britain was essentially a contest for aerial supremacy over southern England, from the Germans' perspective, to facilitate a seaborne invasion of Britain. The battle is officially deemed to have begun on 10 July 1940, by which time Dowding's strength was twenty-five operational Hurricane squadrons and nineteen of Spitfires. Not all of these machines were deployed in southern England, however, as Dowding had to both maintain a substantial reserve and anticipate heavy raids on the industrial north. For example, on 6 July, Fighter Command possessed 871 fighters – but only 644 were operational; on 7 September, Fighter Command's total had increased to 1,161 fighters – of which only 746 were operational. By 16 August, CS airscrews had been fitted to all Spitfires and Hurricanes. More importantly, on 22 August, 611 Squadron received the first Spitfire Mk IIA. This improved Spitfire had a top speed of 370 mph, nearly 50 mph faster than the Hurricane and 15 mph more than the 109. The Mk II's rate of climb was 2,600 feet per minute – 473 feet more than the Mk IA. On 4 September the new Hurricane Mk II was delivered, with a top speed of 342 mph – 28 mph slower than the new Me 109E-4. Of absolutely crucial importance, however, is that the Spitfire Mk IIA's service ceiling was increased to 37,600 feet – 1,600 feet higher than the 109. It was simply impossible to improve the Hurricane significantly further, especially to make it a high-altitude fighter, which it was never going to be. As we have seen, in fighter combat, height, sun and surprise are everything. Frequently the 109s came in very high, just below the stratosphere. Only the Spitfire Mk IIA could meet them either on equal or advantageous terms. This is the most significant development in the Spitfire story thus far.

The Battle of Britain went through distinct phases, dictated by the enemy's changing targets. Channel-bound convoys were hit first, then radar stations, before 11 Group's Sector Stations were pounded. Just when the situation was about to become critical, possibly in retaliation for a nuisance raid on Berlin by Bomber Command, or, more likely, to draw Fighter Command into the air *en masse*, the Luftwaffe began bombing London round the clock. As the phalanxes of enemy bombers droned overhead, discharging their deadly cargoes, many Londoners must have thought that the dreaded 'knock-out' blow had come. Overall, if not quite in reality as legendary as the 'Blitz spirit' of British popular memory, the civilian population reacted stoically. Above, the Hurricanes and Spitfires made interception after interception, inflicting grievous losses on the enemy bomber force on 15 September. By the end of that month, so heavy were Göring's bomber casualties, that the *Kampfgruppen* were forced to assault Britain under the cloak of darkness. By then, the emphasis of the German attack was the British aircraft industry, but this was too late to have any effect upon the conflict's outcome. As autumn weather set in, the day fighting revolved around high-altitude combats involving the fighter forces of both sides, the enemy cleverly including bomb-carrying 109s within their formations, meaning that these incursions could not be ignored. Nonetheless, on 17 September Hitler had indefinitely postponed the proposed invasion of Britain, and such operations were hardly likely to suppress Fighter Command. Strangely, neither air force was defeated in the usual sense by the battle's end, on 31 October 1940: Fighter Command remained an effective force with aerial superiority over its homeland, and the Luftwaffe was not only still a force to be reckoned with but was nightly reducing various British cities to rubble. The fact remains, though, that the Germans failed to wrest aerial supremacy over England from Fighter Command and that was Dowding's victory. By remaining in the war, Britain was ultimately able to become a base from which the Allied liberation of Europe could be launched in 1944. The Spitfires and Hurricanes of Fighter Command, therefore, cost Hitler dearly.

Because the Hurricane was more numerous during the Battle of Britain, it has always been assumed that this type executed much more damage on the enemy – and yet the more shapely and appealing Spitfire walked away with the credit. Recent independent research, by John Alcorn and myself, however, provides a different interpretation. The fact of the matter is that the figures indicate that there was only a narrow margin between the number of enemy aircraft destroyed (not claimed, but confirmed destroyed through rigorous analysis) by each type. On an individual basis, this means that the Spitfire was, according to Alcorn, 2.32 times more effective than the Hurricane, or 1.81 by my own reckoning. Indeed, given the Hurricane's poor high-altitude performance, the Spitfire was required to fly as top cover, protecting the Hawker fighter while it set about the bombers at medium height. Without that protective umbrella, the Hurricanes would virtually always have been at the mercy of Me 109s – which climbed very high over France after take-off and during their journey over the sea. Furthermore, the Spitfire Mk IIA, which was available in numbers by September, possessed a higher service ceiling that the Me 109. The Battle of Britain could not have been won without the Spitfire, contrary to the entrenched Hurricane myth, and, in fact, was won because of it. A full and empirical explanation of this new interpretation appears in my book *How the Spitfire Won the Battle of Britain* (Amberley, 2010), to which I would naturally refer the reader.

The fighter clashes and 'tip 'n' run' raids typical of the Battle of Britain's final phase did not neatly conclude at the end of October. Instead these continued well into the winter, until bad weather finally brought the action to a natural pause in February 1941. Churchill famously described the pivotal year of 1940 as Britain's 'Finest Hour'. It was also that of the Spitfire and Hurricane, the pilots of which were immortalised by Churchill as 'the Few'. The clear performance advantages of the Spitfire, and potential for further development, would see it emerge the following 'season' as the RAF's main fighter: a legend had been confirmed.

Above: 22. A Spitfire Mk IA of 66 Squadron airborne from Duxford in early 1940.

Right: 23. To increase the numbers of operational squadrons available, the Auxiliary Air Force was formed before the war. This is Pilot Officer Denis Adams of the AAF's Spitfire-equipped 611 Squadron 'West Lancashire' Squadron early in 1940. The aircraft is an early Mk IA, still lacking a rear-view mirror. Note the tented accommodation in the background.

Above left: 24. Another AAF unit was 616 'South Yorkshire' Squadron, the Spitfire Mk IAs of which are seen here at Leconfield during early 1940.

Above: 25. The same 616 Squadron Spitfires lined up at dispersal.

Left: 26. In March 1940, Pilot Officer 'Teddy' St Aubyn pranged a 616 Squadron Spitfire at Leconfield while landing at night. The Spitfire was not a good night flying aircraft, for which it was not designed, because of its narrow-track undercarriage. Another Spitfire in the distance appears to have suffered the same fate!

Right: 27. Pilot Officer 'Teddy' St Aubyn: 'All my own work!'

Below: 28. Another 602 Squadron Spitfire at Drem, clearly showing the starting battery plugged in and ready to go.

Below right: 29. The same Spitfire being pushed into position for take-off by the ground crew. Typically, this comprised an engine fitter, airframe and instrument fitter, and armourers.

30. A factory-fresh Spitfire
Mk IA, bearing the code
letters of 609 'West Riding'
Squadron, another AAF
unit, about to undertake
a test flight at Eastleigh,
Southampton in 1940. It was
there that final assembly and
testing took place.

31. A Section of 64 Squadron
Spitfires scramble from
Kenley during the Battle of
Britain.

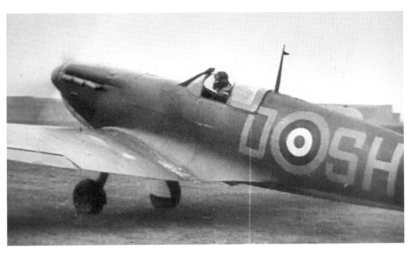

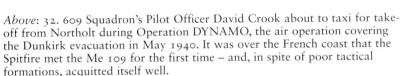

Above: 32. 609 Squadron's Pilot Officer David Crook about to taxi for take-off from Northolt during Operation DYNAMO, the air operation covering the Dunkirk evacuation in May 1940. It was over the French coast that the Spitfire met the Me 109 for the first time – and, in spite of poor tactical formations, acquitted itself well.

Above right: 33. A 64 Squadron Spitfire taxies in. Note the rear-view mirror, in this case faired in to the windscreen.

Right: 34. A flight of 610 'County of Chester' Squadron's Spitfires demonstrate the tight 'vic' formation prescribed by Fighter Command – but which proved disastrous in combat.

Left: 35. A Spitfire of 64 Squadron, flaps down, lands at Kenley during the Battle of Britain.

Below left: 36. Flight Lieutenant Alan Wright of 92 Squadron with his fitter and rigger at Pembrey, August 1940.

Below: 37. Spitfires of 92 Squadron at Pembrey in South Wales, August 1940. The centre aircraft was that of Flight Lieutenant Alan Wright.

Above: 38. A Spitfire of 234 Squadron on finals at St Eval during the Battle of Britain.

Above right: 39. Spitfires being re-armed – a still from an RAF training film.

Right: 40. A 234 Squadron Spitfire having crash-landed at St Eval during the summer of 1940.

Above left: 41. 609 Squadron's Pilot Officer David Crook ready for take-off, Warmwell, August 1940.

Above right: 42. Squadron Leader H. R. L. 'Robin' Hood of 41 Squadron, whose Spitfire also depicted a personal nose-art. The pilot's restraining Sutton Harness can be clearly seen.

Left: 43. Crook's Spitfire being rapidly 'turned around' between combats on *Adlertag*, 13 August 1940.

Above: 44. Flight Lieutenant Ted Graham of 72 Squadron, pictured at Acklington during the Battle of Britain. Noteworthy are the anti-glare night-flying shields fitted fore of the windscreen – designed to prevent the pilot being dazzled by glowing exhaust ports.

Right: 45. Spitfire K9894 of 234 Squadron, in which Pilot Officer Derek Robinson was shot down by Me 109s on 8 August 1940 – the pilot survived the wheels-up crash-landing.

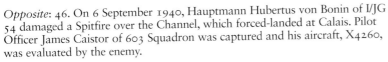

Opposite: 46. On 6 September 1940, Hauptmann Hubertus von Bonin of I/JG 54 damaged a Spitfire over the Channel, which forced-landed at Calais. Pilot Officer James Caistor of 603 Squadron was captured and his aircraft, X4260, was evaluated by the enemy.

Above: 47. Personal photography on service installations was prohibited, but a surprising number of snapshots were taken by proud airmen posing with their aircraft. This dawn photograph was taken at Kirton-in-Lindsey of 222 Squadron's Spitfire Mk IA P9318 and Pilot Officer Laurie Whitbread by Sergeant Reg Johnson.

Above right: 48. Pilot Officer Whitbread then returned the favour, photographing Sergeant Johnson beside the same Spitfire. Interestingly, the rear-view mirror is housed within the windscreen assembly.

Right: 49. Spitfires of 222 and 603 Squadron at Hornchurch in early September 1940. 'XT-M' is the aircraft in which Pilot Officer Richard Hillary, author of *The Last Enemy*, was shot down in flames on 3 September 1940. Note the steamroller repairing bomb damage.

Above left: 50. 222 Squadron was heavily engaged flying from Hornchurch during the Battle of Britain. Like 11 Group's other Sector Stations it was heavily bombed – this is one of the Squadron's wrecked Spitfires after a particularly heavy raid on 31 August 1940.

Above: 51. A 222 Squadron Spitfire being over-flown by an Anson at Hornchurch. The square patch on the wing was yellow, and changed colour indicating a gas attack.

Left: 52. Another surreptitious airfield snapshot: Pilot Officer Eric 'Sawn Off' Lock, who would become one of the Battle of Britain's top aces, with his 41 Squadron Spitfire Mk IA at Catterick.

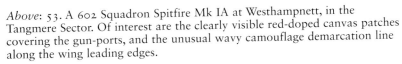

Above: 53. A 602 Squadron Spitfire Mk IA at Westhampnett, in the Tangmere Sector. Of interest are the clearly visible red-doped canvas patches covering the gun-ports, and the unusual wavy camouflage demarcation line along the wing leading edges.

Above right: 54. Pilot Officer Osgood 'Pedro' Hanbury with a cannon-shell-damaged Spitfire Mk IA X4389 of 602 Squadron, sometime between 3 September and 31 October 1940. As so often happened, given the administrative chaos of the time, there appears to be no record of this aircraft being so damaged.

Right: 55. 222 Squadron fitter Joe Crowshaw sat in Spitfire P9323. This aircraft was shot down over the Isle of Sheppey on 31 August 1940.

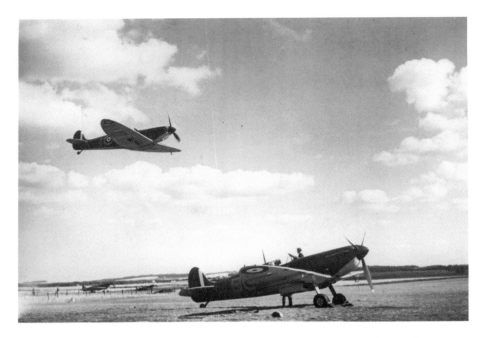

Opposite: 56. A postcard produced by 66 Squadron, showing its Spitfires and personnel at Gravesend during the Battle of Britain. The Spitfire below right is that of the CO, Squadron Leader Athol Forbes, and displays his squadron leader's rank pennant. At top right is Flight Lieutenant Ken Gillies, whose Spitfire shows another faired-in rear-view mirror. This appears to be a more common feature on Spitfires at this time than is perhaps acknowledged today.

Above: 57. 19 Squadron's Mk IBs were replaced by machine-gun-armed Mk IAs. Here Sergeant Jenning's overflies another Squadron aircraft at Fowlmere in September 1940.

Right: 58. A pilot of 74 Squadron at Hornchurch, the photograph showing the 'trolley acc' plugged in.

Above left: 59. Sergeant Jennings prepares to scramble for the camera, his engine already running.

Above right: 60. Sergeant Jennings and Spitfire Mk IA X4474; both are pictured in their natural environment.

Left: 61. Sergeant Jennings takes off from Fowlmere in QV-I, X4474.

Right: 62. Another posed photograph: back at Fowlmere, armourer Fred Roberts re-arms Sergeant Jennings's Spitfire.

Below: 63. The Mk Spitfire IA of 19 Squadron's CO, Squadron Leader Brian Lane. Of interest is the unusual outsize fuselage roundel and yellow propeller spinner. This machine ultimately perished with its pilot in a Scottish flying accident.

Below right: 64. 616 Squadron also operated from Fowlmere in September 1940, while participating in 12 Group Wing operations. Here one of that Squadron's Mk IAs prepares for flight; note the 'chocks' in place.

Opposite: 65. On 5 September 1940, 19 Squadron's Pilot Officer Eric Burgoyne was attacked by an Me 109 over Hornchurch; this is the result of being hit by 20 mm cannon fire. It is often said that the Hurricane could absorb great damage and keep flying – the photographic evidence suggests that, contrary to popular belief, so could the Spitfire. Interestingly this aircraft's individual serial number, P9391, appears painted across the tail-top, rather than on the usual after-fuselage.

Above: 66. Pilot Officer Bob Beardsley of 41 Squadron at Hornchurch, whose Spitfire Mk IA shows to good effect the armoured windscreen, reflector gun sight and externally mounted rear-view mirror.

Above right: 67. Sergeant Terry Healey of 41 Squadron with his Spitfire at Hornchurch – victory tallies have been chalked on the cockpit-side – including two RAF roundels and a question mark! Identity of the 'wag' raising the 'two fingered salute' is unknown!

Right: 68. The small factory of Vickers-Supermarine at Woolston was unable to cope with producing sufficient Spitfires. Consequently Lord Nuffield was charged with overseeing the opening of a new Spitfire plant at Castle Bromwich, which applied the mass-production methods of the automotive industry to making Spitfires.

Top left: 69. Sergeant Terry Healey of 41 Squadron confers with his armourers at Hornchurch.

Bottom left: 70. Another view of Spitfires being made at Castle Bromwich. Surprisingly, the Luftwaffe never mounted a major raid against this crucial target.

Left: 71. The first Spitfires produced at Castle Bromwich were the new Mk IIAs, which reached the Squadrons during the Battle of Britain. An improvement over the previous two-pitch propeller was the Dowty Rotol Constant Speed Airscrew, seen here with its broader blades, made of laminated wood covered in a plastic-like material called Jablo. This example, of 19 Squadron, was snapped at Fowlmere with Czech pilot Frantiszek Hradil – he was later shot down and killed over Southend.

Opposite: 72. Squadron Leader Lane's Mk IIA at Fowlmere, displaying his rank pennant. This machine was fitted not only with the common external rear-view mirror but also with locally improvised side-mounted mirrors.

Left: 73. Throughout the war, the Spitfire was used for propaganda purposes, inspiring people to support the war effort. This is a Royal Australian Air Force recruiting poster – featuring a victorious Spitfire.

Above: 74. Towards the end of the Battle of Britain, a 'Jim Crow' high-altitude reconnaissance flight was formed, operating out of Hawkinge. Although of poor quality, this is an extremely rare snapshot of one of those Mk IIAs.

Above: 75. The cash generated by Spitfire Funds did not, in reality, have any effect on Spitfire production, but nonetheless served a valuable purpose by getting the Home Front involved. The activity peaked during the Battle of Britain, and by early 1941 Spitfires with serial numbers designated as being 'presentation' aircraft were beginning to appear. The donor's name was applied to the fuselage in yellow paint at the factory, where the machines were photographed for publicity purposes. This is a Mk IIA, P7925, 'Weston Super Mare', which was built at Castle Bromwich in February 1941.

Above right: 76. An early presentation Spitfire, a Mk I, R7058, was appropriately named 'RJ Mitchell'.

Right: 77. In the winter of 1940/41, various Mk II airframes were upgraded to the new Mk V status. This is one of those aircraft, P8714, the presentation Spitfire 'Spirit of Warrington II'. This machine failed to return from operations of 15 October 1941.

— SUTTON IN ASHFIELD SPITFIRE —
"SILVER SNIPE"

THE FUND REALISED £5,126 IN EIGHT WEEKS AND WAS PROMOTED BY:—
A. FARNSWORTH, J. GASTON, H.S. SHACKLOCK, J. WADE, J.G. WALTON, R. WOODSIDE
SEPTEMBER 1940

Opposite: 78. In September 1940, the Sutton-in-Ashfield Spitfire Fund raised £5,126 in just eight weeks. This was the result: Mk I R7193, 'Silver Snipe'. This aircraft later went to Canada for photographic trials.

Above left: 79. The Battle of Britain officially ended on 31 October 1940, although the fighter forces of both sides clashed over southern England and the Channel until February 1941. By night, of course, the Germans rained down bombs upon British cities, not least Coventry. Fighter Command, however, prepared for the daylight battles of the 'season' ahead. Squadrons were rotated so that battle-weary units could rest, re-fit, and train new pilots. 65 Squadron, for example, had been hotly engaged during the summer of 1940, but on 26 February 1941 flew north, to Kirton, exchanging its new Mk IIs with the old Mk IAs of 616 Squadron, which relieved the unit at Tangmere. This is Sergeant Johnson (right) of 65 Squadron, pictured with one of those Mk IAs at Kirton, with an unknown Polish pilot. In fact, the aircraft has the Polish Air Force chequered red-and-white-square insignia applied below the windscreen. The aircraft also has one wing under-surface painted black, which was a camouflage scheme used between 27 November 1940 and 22 April 1941.

Above right: 80. Pilot Officer Jack Strang, a New Zealander serving with 65 Squadron, seated in a Mk IA at Kirton during the winter of 1940. Unusually given this date, this machine still has an un-faired radio mast and no rear-view mirror whatsoever. Strang was later reported missing in action.

3

THE UNTOLD STORY: 1941

Soon after the Battle of Britain, in what remains a controversial decision, Dowding and Park were replaced by Air Chief Marshal Sholto Douglas and Air Vice-Marshal Leigh-Mallory as Commander-in-Chief and Commander of 11 Group respectively. These men had opposing ideas on the tactical employment of day fighters. Dowding and Park believed that their forces should be carefully preserved and committed to battle in small numbers. Douglas and Leigh-Mallory argued that fighters should be deployed *en masse*, in so-called 'Big Wings' of three squadrons. This debate erupted during the Battle of Britain, spearheaded by Leigh-Mallory's 12 Group, covering the industrial Midlands, and was the brainchild of an Acting Squadron Leader: Douglas Bader. Inspirational and enormously admired for being a double amputee, the fact remains that Bader was wrong regarding massed fighter tactics; again, I would refer the reader to either my work *The Few* or *Bader's Duxford Fighters: The Big Wing Controversy* (see bibliography). Nonetheless, given their offensive nature, these tactics were to dominate Fighter Command's approach to the New Year. Douglas and Leigh-Mallory were keen 'reach out' and 'lean into France'.

From the outset they propounded an offensive strategy, and from March 1941 onwards re-organised Fighter Command into Wings of three squadrons, each based at a Sector Station. Significantly for our purposes, by the beginning of 1941, all of 11 Group's squadrons – being the front line – were equipped with the Spitfire Mk II, the Hurricane having been relegated to a secondary day fighter role with 10, 12 and 13 Groups, and used as a stopgap night fighter.

By this time, the Spitfire had cannon. The experimental Mk IBs issued to 19 Squadron during the Battle of Britain were so unsuccessful that ultimately the pilots lost all confidence in their aircraft, which were replaced by standard machine-gun-armed Mk IAs. By adding blisters to the wings, like the Me 109E, the ammunition drum was eventually accommodated and the weapon mounted correctly, thus resolving the jamming of spent shell cases. Two machine-guns were retained in each wing, providing the pilot with the advantages of either firing both types of weapon simultaneously, or selecting one or the other by way of a button on the control column. Each cannon, however, weighed 96 lbs, excluding ammunition, and so it made perfect sense to attach them to the Spitfire Mk II, those aircraft with this combination fire-power being designated Mk IIB. Even so, it transpired that the Mk II's Merlin XII was not powerful enough to cope with the extra weight, leading to development of the Merlin 45 and Spitfire Mk V. This new fighter had a top speed of 359 mph at 25,000 feet, which altitude it reached in eight minutes, and could achieve a maximum ceiling of 35,000 feet. By May 1941, the Spitfire Mk V was reaching the fighter squadrons in numbers.

Fighter Command employed various types of operations, including so-called 'Rhubarbs', entailing pairs of Spitfires streaking low across the Channel to avoid radar detection and attacking targets of opportunity, 'Ramrods', which were similar but involving more aircraft and delivered against a specific target, fighter sweeps and the more complex 'Circus'. In the latter, a small number of medium bombers were tasked with attacking targets in Northern France and escorted by hundreds of Spitfires. The inclusion of bombers meant that the enemy would be unable to ignore these incursions. The intention was that the massed RAF fighter formations would then destroy the German fighters piecemeal. The record shows, however, that this was not the case. As there were no targets in occupied France of great strategic importance to the Germans, the Luftwaffe could choose carefully when to engage. Wisely, the enemy only attacked when the tactical situation was favourable to them. The Germans now had the much improved Me 109F, an altogether more curvaceous and elliptical design than the old Emil, and which was a match for the Spitfire Mk V. Again, the enemy pilots climbed very high, diving out of the sun in fast passes. Given the benefits of fuel injection, the Germans' standard evasive tactic was to dive at full boost. This manoeuvre produced a stream of black smoke from the exhaust ports, leading many an RAF pilot to believe that his target

had been hit and destroyed. In reality, the enemy machine would frequently pull up either in or below cloud, undamaged. We know now that the more fighters are engaged the greater will be the over-claiming factor, due to the speed and confusion involved. Moreover, as the RAF was fighting at high altitude, often above cloud, and over France, Intelligence Officers had no wrecks to visit on the ground. Claims during 1941, therefore, were unavoidably hugely inflated – providing a completely false impression of the 'Non-Stop Offensive's' progress. Throughout this time of cross-Channel operations, many experienced fighter leaders were lost, ironically including the Tangmere Wing's Wing Commander Douglas Bader, shot down accidentally by one of his own pilots during a massive dogfight over St Omer. Such men Fighter Command could ill afford to lose. By the end of the 'season', Fighter Command was losing the battle by a ratio of over 2:1.

On 22 June 1941 Hitler invaded the Soviet Union. Thereafter Britain was under increasing pressure from Stalin to provide aid and, in particular, open a second front. The latter was impossible. The only real way to demonstrate support was by continuing with the aerial campaign over Northern France by day and Germany by night. The objective was to force the Germans to reinforce the Channel coast with fighter units from Russia, thus relieving the pressure on that front. This never happened. After the Battle of Britain German fighter units dispersed to other theatres, leaving just JG 26 and JG 2 on the Channel coast. These experienced and skilfully led units literally held the fort, and no German reinforcements were required. In one respect, though, the Spitfire pilots had made progress. There was still no unified approach regarding tactical squadron formations, squadrons still making their own individual arrangements as per their commander's preference. At Tangmere in May 1941, Wing Commander Bader, acting upon a suggestion by Pilot Officer Hugh Dundas, had started experimenting with a section of four aircraft, like the German *schwarm*. Once perfected, the superiority of what the RAF called either the 'Finger Four' or 'Cross-over Four', was abundantly apparent; soon, this became standard operating procedure throughout Fighter Command.

Then, in September 1941, a new menace appeared in dangerous French skies: the Focke-Wulf (FW) 190. The performance of this enemy machine was phenomenal. The aircraft's fourteen-cylinder, 1,700 hp, BMW radial engine provided a maximum speed of 312 mph at 15,000 feet; with a one minute override boost it could exceed 400 mph. With a maximum service ceiling of 35,000 feet, the 190 could reach 26,000 feet – the height around which most combats were commonly fought – in twelve minutes, and was extremely manoeuvrable. By comparison, the Spitfire Mk V's maximum speed at 20,000 feet was 371 mph. It was unable to operate efficiently above 25,000 feet, by which altitude the top speed had dropped to 359 mph and took fifteen minutes to reach. Significantly, for the first time, an enemy fighter could out-turn the Spitfire. As RAF losses mounted, for the first time Spitfire pilots lost confidence in their aircraft, their radius of penetration being restricted to the French coast. The year 1941 was not a good one for Fighter Command, but on the world stage the balance of power had shifted: on 7 December 1941, Japan made a surprise attack on the American Pacific Fleet at Pearl Harbor. With America now in the war at last, and Hitler fighting on two fronts, Britain's reward for remaining free and continuing war against Germany, although still far off, was nonetheless in sight.

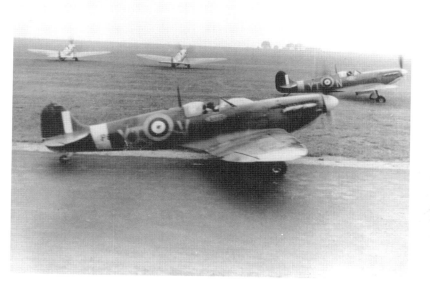

Above: 81. On 29 November 1941, 65 Squadron returned to Tangmere for another tour of duty in the front line. Here a section of the Squadron's Spitfires taxi for take-off.

Opposite: 82. A Spitfire Mk IA, of 65 'East India' Squadron, at Kirton in April 1941. The 'sky' band around the after-fuselage indicates that the aircraft is a day fighter.

83. Another Spitfire Mk IA at Kirton, N3284, early in 1941– without a rear-view mirror.

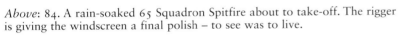

Above: 84. A rain-soaked 65 Squadron Spitfire about to take-off. The rigger is giving the windscreen a final polish – to see was to live.

Above right: 85. A 65 Squadron Mk II being serviced out on a soggy Westhampnett.

Right: 86. A close-up of a 65 Squadron Mk IIA at Westhampnett in late 1941.

Above left: 87. A 65 Squadron Mk II, showing off to good effect the CS propeller and 'fishtail' exhausts.

Above right: 88. A prominent identification feature on the Mk II was the bulge seen adjacent to the propeller, accommodating the Coffman starter system, which fired by way of a cartridge – precluding the use of an accumulator trolley.

Left: 89. The same Spitfire, giving a closer view of the pear-shaped Coffman blister.

Above: 90. The tube shown and the armoured windscreen's base was used to pump glycol onto the glass at high altitude, thus preventing it freezing over.

Above right: 91. 66 Squadron flew from Exeter in early 1941, one of the Squadron's Mk IIs seen here on trestles, having its guns harmonised. This is P7843, 'Aldergrove', presented by the *Belfast Telegraph* Spitfire Fund.

Right: 92. 66 Squadron was attacked at night while at Exeter, this Spitfire being damaged.

Above left: 93. By May 1941 the cannon-armed Spitfire Mk II was reaching the squadrons, this being a fine study of an aircraft belonging to 92 Squadron.

Above: 94. Early Mk Vs were upgraded Mk I airframes, this being one of them, still fitted with the two-pitch propeller. The cannons are shown to good effect as this aircraft approaches on finals.

Left: 95. Another Spitfire damaged in the attack on Exeter – presumably, as the nose is covered in tarpaulin, it was in the process of being serviced.

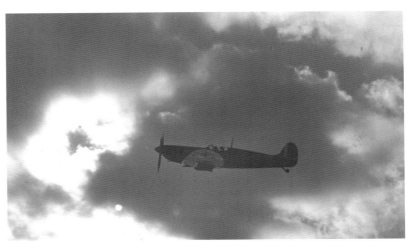

Above: 96. A Spitfire Mk V of 616 Squadron being overhauled. Almost immediately the Mk V became obsolete, being completely outclassed in September 1941 by the FW 190.

Above right: 97. This presentation Spitfire is another upgraded Mk IA, R7195, 'Holmewood', one of four aircraft presented by the High Sheriff of Cambridge. This machine had a long service life, during which Pilot Officer Phil Archer of 92 Squadron at Biggin Hill – where this photograph was taken – destroyed two Me 109s in June and July 1941. During the latter combat 'Holmewood' was damaged and Archer was wounded. It was eventually lost on a weather reconnaissance flight over Le Touquet in 1944. Protruding from the wing blister is the mechanism used to load the 20 mm ammunition drum.

Right: 98. An evocative Charles Brown study of Spitfire R6823.

Above left: 99. Pilots of 118 Squadron with a Spitfire Mk VB at Ibsley in Hampshire – note the rubber condom-like sleeve over the cannon barrel, to keep the barrel dirt-free.

Above: 100. Pilot Officer Oldnall with 65 Squadron's 'Sind V', one of seven aircraft presented by the people of this Indian province (now in West Pakistan), P7836. The aircraft sports an unofficial nose-art – a parrot – and was taken at Tangmere between 14 and 26 February 1941.

Left: 101. 501 Squadron was also based at Ibsley in 1941, flying Spitfire Mk IIs. Here the 'Chiefy', Flight Sergeant Lewis, senior NCO in charge of 'A' Flight's ground crew, is pictured with Pilot Officer Walter Milne.

Above: 102. The RAF airfield and Spitfire flying scenes in Howard's film were produced at Ibsley, featuring the pilots and aircraft of 118 and 501 Squadrons in 1941.

Above right: 103. Howard ducks below the wing of a Mk IIA – the Coffman blister of which appears somewhat battered!

Right: 104. One of the scenes featured an airfield under attack and a crash-landing – performed here by the CO of 118 Squadron, Squadron Leader Frank Howell.

Above left: 105. Howard directs from the wrecked Spitfire's cockpit, while Howell, hands on hips, considers the scene with the sunglasses-wearing Niven. This is yet another presentation aircraft, Mk VB P8789. It was not really destroyed, though it was on 1 June 1942, when Flight Sergeant Ron Stillwell abandoned the machine over the Channel due to engine failure. Fortunately the pilot was rescued from the water after two hours by a 277 Squadron Walrus – also designed by R. J. Mitchell.

Above: 106. A 118 Squadron Mk IIA, 'Sinaboong', P8376, at Ibsley in 1941. This Spitfire was destroyed in a mid-air collision over Hampshire later that year.

Left: 107. Flight Lieutenant Peter Howard-Williams of 118 Squadron, sat on wing, with members of his Flight and personal Mk IIA, named after his girlfriend 'Shelia'. All of this pilot's Spitfires were also adorned with a black Labrador's head silhouette within a white box – this can just be seen beneath the windscreen.

Right: 108. Howard-Williams with the same aircraft – note that the serial number has been partially obscured by the day fighter band, and parachute positioned on the wing-tip.

Below: 109. One of the first Wing Leaders appointed, in March 1941, was the legless Wing Commander Douglas Bader, who chose Tangmere, near Chichester. This is Mk IIA P7966, 'Manxman', bearing the Wing Leader's initials, 'DB'.

Below right: 110. Spitfire 'Dogsbody' was the first to be fitted with a colour cine-gun camera, made by Kodak, which was installed in the field at Westhampnett during the early summer of 1941. Of great interest is the Wing Leader's nose-art: Hitler being kicked in the backside by a flying boot, similar to the artwork applied to Bader's 242 Squadron Hurricane during the Battle of Britain.

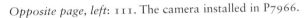

Opposite page, left: 111. The camera installed in P7966.

Opposite page, right: 112. A Spitfire cine-gun camera installation (in a different aircraft) viewed from above. These were of great value to Intelligence Officers in analysing aerial combats.

Above: 113. A 'Finger Four' of 616 Squadron Spitfires take off from Westhampnett, bound no doubt for France. The photographer, Norman Jackson, was the same airman who pictured the camera being fitted to P7966 and visited the airfield for that official purpose.

Above right: 114. The Spitfire Mk VB, BL584, of Flight Lieutenant Denis Crowley-Milling of 610 Squadron, at Westhampnett in 1941. Note the broader-based airscrew common to the Mk V.

Right: 115. Crowley-Milling's fitter and rigger with the same Spitfire.

Above left: 116. The other Tangmere Wing squadron that summer was 145, based at Merston. This is Flight Lieutenant Newlin's personal Mk IIA.

Above: 117. Sergeant Frank Twitchett's so-called 145 Squadron 'War Horse', P7980.

Left: 118. An unofficial air-to-air snapshot taken by Sergeant Twitchett of 145 Squadron's Sergeant Johnson up from Merston in the summer of 1941.

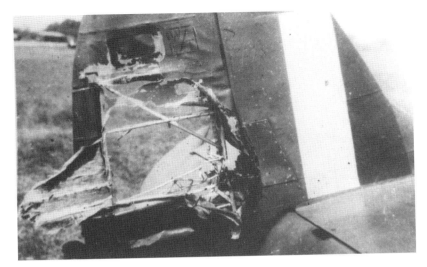

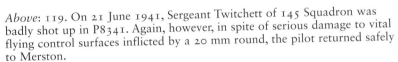

Above: 119. On 21 June 1941, Sergeant Twitchett of 145 Squadron was badly shot up in P8341. Again, however, in spite of serious damage to vital flying control surfaces inflicted by a 20 mm round, the pilot returned safely to Merston.

Above right: 120. On 5 May 1941, Pilot Officer Lionel 'Buck' Casson of 616 Squadron was attacked a Ju 88 over Littlehampton but was himself shot down by return fire. He baled out of this aircraft, P7753, 'Pampero I'.

Right: 121. Flying accidents of one type or another were not uncommon. This Spitfire of 610 Squadron was written off in such an incident occurring at Acklington.

Opposite: 122. When the time came to upgrade to a Spitfire Mk V, Wing Commander Bader preferred the Mk VA, which was only armed with machine-guns. This gave a better spread of fire than the cannon, which required accurate shooting – something Bader considered largely beyond the average squadron pilot. Bader is pictured here after returning from a sweep in Mk VA W3185. The Tangmere Wing Leader fell victim to so-called 'friendly fire' in this aircraft during a confused combat over St Omer on 9 August 1941. He spent the remainder of the war as a prisoner.

Above: 123. The pilot accidentally responsible for opening fire on 'Dogsbody' was Pilot Officer Casson, who was shot down near Calais while returning home. This is the remains of his Spitfire, Mk VB W3458. After crash-landing, Casson ignited an incendiary device situated in the cockpit, known as a 'Portfire', thus depriving the enemy of capturing this aircraft intact. Casson also saw out the war as a prisoner. For the full story of this fascinating action, please see my *Spitfire Voices: Life as a Spitfire Pilot in the Words of the Veterans*.

Above right: 124. A spectacular air-to-air photograph of Squadron Leader Jan Zumbach's Spitfire Mk V. Zumbach was the CO of Northolt's 303 Squadron, and this livery was recently applied to the Battle of Britain Memorial Flight's airworthy Mk VB, AB910.

Right: 125. Fighter Command's offensive daylight operations over Northern France in 1941 were often complex operations involving hundreds of aircraft. These are the Spitfire Mk Vs of Northolt's Polish Fighter Wing taking off on one such operation that fateful year.

Above left: 126. Pilot Officer Stanislaw Wandzilak of 308 Squadron prepares for a sweep. The Polish marking was usually painted on the engine cowling, but appears here in an unusual location.

Above: 127. The Polish General Sikorski visits 308 Squadron at Heston in 1941 to decorate pilots. In the background is Mk VB AA735, 'ZF-N', illustrating the Polish emblem applied in its usual place.

Left: 128. A 308 Squadron Spitfire Mk VB returns to Northolt safely.

Above: 129. Pilot Officer Roger Boulding of 74 Squadron, pictured at Gravesend in spring 1941 with Spitfire P8394, 'Gibraltar'.

Right: 130. Pilot Officer Stanislaw Stabrowski with a 308 Squadron Spitfire at Northolt, providing a close-up of the Polish marking.

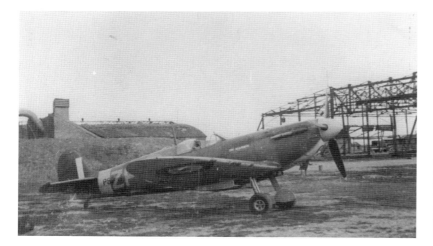

Above left: 131. Another 74 Squadron machine, Mk IIA P8047, 'The Malverns', at Manston in 1941.

Above: 132. Pilots of 74 Squadron at Gravesend with Spitfire Mk IIA P8388, 'Black Vanities'.

Left: 133. An unknown pilot of 74 Squadron with Mk IIA P8261 in May 1941. This aircraft survived the war, being struck off charge three days after VE Day.

Above: 134. A 74 Squadron Spitfire, the serial number of which is unfortunately obscured by the squadron code letters, making identification impossible. The canopy appears shattered, however, possibly by enemy fire.

Above right: 135. Another uncaptioned photograph from the album of 74 Squadron pilot Bob Poulton, the serial number of this aircraft, either a Mk IA or, more likely, a Mk IIA fitted with a two-pitch propeller, being exasperatingly obscured by the personnel posing with the Spitfire. The aircraft has obviously been forced-landed.

Right: 136. Pilot Officer Bob Beardsley of 41 Squadron pictured at Catterick in a Mk IIA – this is not a presentation Spitfire, but named after the pilot's wife.

Above left: 137. Sergeant John McAdam of 41 Squadron at Hornchurch, pictured with a Mk IIA. The rather bulbous spinner of the Rotol propeller is clearly shown.

Above: 138. Sergeant McAdam in his 41 Squadron Mk IIA. Behind him, the pilot's head armour can be seen attached to the black leather headrest, and the sheet of armour plate protecting the pilot's back can also be seen. Another sheet of plate was positioned between the instrument panel and fuel tank. Sadly, McAdam was reported missing over the Channel shortly after this snapshot was taken.

Left: 139. Sergeant Mitchell of 41 Squadron, in a Spitfire Mk IIA at Catterick in 1941. This aircraft has an unusual blister in the perspex canopy, usually seen on Photographic Reconnaissance Spitfires.

Above left: 140. Pilot Officer Stevens of 19 Squadron at Fowlmere in 1941, with Spitfire Mk IIA 'The Red Rose'

Above right: 141. 19 Squadron's Sergeant David Cox's Spitfire Mk IIA, called 'Pat' after his wife.

Right: 142. Sergeant Cox pictured with 19 Squadron's 'Armagh' in June 1941.

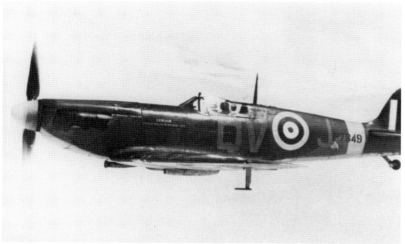

Above left: 143. Squadron Leader Walter Lawson, who succeeded Squadron Leader Brian Lane as CO of 19 Squadron, airborne in 'Armagh'. Later transferred to the US Army Air Corps, this Spitfire was ultimately destroyed in a mid-air collision over Shropshire.

Above & left: 144, 145. Spitfire Mk IIAs of 19 Squadron's 'A' Flight over Cambridge in 1941.

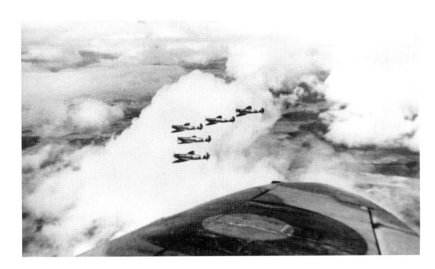

This page: 146, 147 & 148. Spitfire Mk IIAs of 19 Squadron's 'A' Flight over Cambridge in 1941.

Above left: 149. An early Spitfire Mk VB of 504 Squadron visiting the glider training school at RAF Shobdon in Herefordshire during 1941.

Above: 150. The pilot's control column in a Spitfire Mk VB. Accidental operation of the gun button on the ground is prevented by a protective plate warning that the aircraft's weapons are 'Loaded'.

Left: 151. Yet another presentation Spitfire, this time Mk VB P8714, 'Spirit of Warrington I'. On 15 October 1941, this aircraft was destroyed over Le Havre by an Me 109. The pilot, Sergeant Ray Barnett of 234 Squadron, was reported missing.

Above: 152. A Spitfire Mk VB under fire from *Oberleutnant* Gerhard Schöpfel of III/JG 26 on 26 June 1941.

Above right: 153. Senior RAF and Army officers at the handover ceremony of Spitfire Mk IIA P8044, 'First Canadian Division' to 41 Squadron.

Right: 154. Two 72 Squadron Spitfires being prepared for a sweep over France in 1941, while a third taxies for take-off; did it return, I wonder?

Previous spread, left: 155. Pilot Officer Peter Brown of 41 Squadron aloft in P8044.

Previous spread, right: 156. A new Spitfire Mk VB has its guns harmonised at Biggin Hill in 1941.

Above left: 157. A superb study of a flight of Spitfire Mk VBs.

Above: 158. A Spitfire Mk VB of 616 Squadron being overhauled at Kingscliffe.

Left: 159. Spitfire Mk VB AA879, 'Manchester Civil Defender', of 616 Squadron. This machine was flown regularly by Flight Lieutenant Johnnie Johnson – who became the RAF's top-scoring fighter pilot of the Second World War. The kneeling armourers prepare to load belts of machine-gun bullets, while the 'plumber' on the wing deals with the 20 mm cannon ammunition drum.

Above left: 160. Flight Lieutenant Johnson's 616 Squadron Spitfire Mk VB, AA879, being re-armed.

Above right: 161. 616 Squadron armourers feed belts of bullets into an ammunition box, prior to re-arming the Spitfire.

Right: 162. Another example of the Spitfire's resilience to cannon fire: Spitfire Mk VB AB930 of 308 Squadron, which Sergeant Jan Okroj nursed back from France on 20 September 1941. Pilot Officer Franek Surma was reported missing in this aircraft on Circus 110, Fighter Command's last major offensive operation of 1941.

4

SALVATION: 1942

Naturally there was great pressure for Spitfire performance to be increased. The answer was the Spitfire Mk IX, which was essentially a Mk V airframe, the nose of which was slightly extended to accommodate the new Merlin 61. With a top speed of 409 mph at 28,000 feet, a maximum service ceiling of 43,000 feet, and a climbing speed of 4,000 feet per minute, this was the fighter that Fighter Command so desperately required. In July 1942, comparison trials were undertaken between a Spitfire Mk IX and a recently captured FW 190. The result was favourable to the new Spitfire, with which the RAF squadrons began re-equipping the following month. On 30 July, the Mk IX achieved its first success over the 190, and, on 12 September destroyed an enemy high-altitude reconnaissance bomber at 43,000 feet. Suddenly morale was restored, and the RAF pilots were once again able to wage war on a fair footing. Indeed, the Mk IX became the most numerous of all twenty-four Spitfire marks, with a total of 5,710 being built.

The Spitfire, however, had been designed as a short-range defensive interceptor. It was not created to fulfil the role of a cross-Channel offensive fighter, or bomber escort. The operations of 1941, however, had seen the Spitfire pilots doing just this. By the spring of 1942, the American 8th Air Force was operating from bases in England, determined to perfect accurate daylight bombing of targets within Germany itself. The problem was that the Spitfire Mk IX's range, even with a 30-gallon auxiliary fuel tank, was only 980 miles. This meant that the American bombers could only be escorted so far over enemy occupied territory before the escorting fighters had to turn back, re-fuel and meet their charges when homeward bound. Of course, the period of time when the bomber formations were unprotected was when the enemy fighters struck. From this point onwards, the lack of a long-range fighter became of increasing concern to the Allies – a role later fulfilled by American fighters such as the P-51 Mustang, P-38 Lightning and P-47 Thunderbolt.

Control of the Mediterranean was also bitterly contested during the first half of the war. Geographically the key to that theatre was the tiny island of Malta, on the supply route to North Africa where British forces were engaged with those of Germany and

Italy. For three weeks in 1940, in fact, the island's defence was undertaken by three antiquated Gladiator biplanes, known as 'Faith', 'Hope' and 'Charity'. At the end of June, four Hurricanes arrived and throughout the following month these seven fighters resisted the best efforts of some 200 enemy aircraft based in Sicily. So furiously did the defenders fight that eventually the Italians, like the Germans over England, were forced to operate only at night. More Hurricanes arrived but by March 1942 the Italians had been joined by superior Luftwaffe units and the contest was at its height. That month fifteen Spitfires flew off the aircraft carrier HMS *Eagle*, landing at Takali. Within three days the Spitfires had destroyed their first enemy aircraft. In an effort to destroy the Spitfire force, Takali was bombed repeatedly: by 2 April not one complete section of Spitfires was operational. Indeed, the defenders thought themselves lucky if they could field six fighters at any one time, two for airfield defence and four to intercept. Incredibly, sometimes the RAF pilots had no ammunition, it being in such short supply, but the Germans could never be sure, so always treated the Spitfires with respect.

On 15 April 1942, Malta was awarded the George Cross, and five days later forty-seven more Spitfires reach the besieged island. Following intense attacks, a day later only eighteen Spitfires were serviceable; two days later none were airworthy. For some unknown reason, however, the Luftwaffe then made another classic tactical blunder, as it had at a crucial moment in the Battle of Britain, and eased off the pressure. This enabled sixty-four Spitfires, flying off the aircraft carriers USS *Wasp* and HMS *Eagle*, to get through to Malta. A clever system was devised to rapidly turn the aircraft around, to prevent them being caught on the ground: six Spitfires were up again within just six minutes of landing! By 23 October, Rommel had been defeated in the desert, and soon, after the Americans landed, the Allies were rolling up North Africa from both directions. The defence of Malta has rightly become legendary, but Spitfire operations from the island are important for another reason: it was from Malta that Spitfire fighter-bombers first flew, two 500-lb bombs carried beneath their wings, attacking enemy airfields in Sicily. This was another role not envisaged by the Spitfire's designer, indicating the airframe's strength and versatility. Spitfires had also flown in the Desert Air Force during the North African Campaign, and many of these units now gathered on Malta ready for the push into Europe via Sicily. From Malta the Spitfire wings swept over Sicily in an attempt to bring German fighters to battle, in much the same way as was happening over Northern France.

163. In addition to individual aircraft there were also 'Presentation Squadrons'. These are the Spitfire Mk VBs of 91 'Nigeria' Squadron lined up at Hawkinge in 1942.

Above: 164. Squadron Leader Bobby Oxpring with his 'Nigeria' Squadron pilots. By now, Fighter Command was a multinational entity, including not only free pilots from the occupied lands but also many from the Commonwealth countries.

Above right: 165. For the first half of 1942, Fighter Command's front-line squadrons remained equipped with the Spitfire Mk VB – which was completely outclassed by the FW 190. In May 1942, 65 Squadron returned to 11 Group for another front-line tour. This is Pilot Officer Vic Lowson in his Mk VB, the serial number of which is obscured by a fresh coat of camouflage. Lowson was reported missing over the North Sea on 21 July, the victim of flak during a low-level attack on Zeebrugge.

Right: 166. Just how many pilots could a Spitfire's nose accommodate? Here is the answer! In 1942, 152 Squadron served in Northern Ireland, flying Mk IIs, which were relegated to the second division.

Above left: 167. A Spitfire takes off from Rednal in Shropshire, the home of 61 Operational Training Unit.

Above: 168. Unofficial nose-art was popular. Here the Belgian Squadron Leader Michel Donnet poses with his Red Indian-emblazoned Mk V.

Left: 169. A Spitfire Mk VB of the Czech 310 Squadron being refuelled from a bowser.

Above: 170. A Spitfire Mk VB of 310 Squadron, 'trolley acc' plugged in. The stub adjacent to the cannon was to facilitate fitting an extra weapon.

Above right: 171. Spitfire Mk VBs of 310 Squadron taxi for take-off.

Right: 172. A 310 Spitfire Mk VB gets airborne.

Above left: 173. In June 1941, Squadron Leader Peter Brothers was posted to Baginton, to form 457 (Australian) Squadron. One of the Squadron's Mk IIs takes off in 1942.

Above right: 174. Snapped from another Spitfire, Squadron Leader Brothers leads 457 Squadron on a training flight over Scotland in 1942.

Left: 175. 457 Squadron Spitfires in flight, 1942.

Above left: 176. 457 Squadron Spitfires in flight, 1942.

Above right: 177. A crashed Spitfire of 457 Squadron, from the album of Air Commodore Brothers. Unfortunately no details were recorded, but the snapshot provides a rare glimpse of the propeller's internal mechanism.

Right: 178. A Spitfire Mk VB of 19 Squadron's 'Killer Section' at Perranporth in 1942. (Roger Henderson, via Cablac)

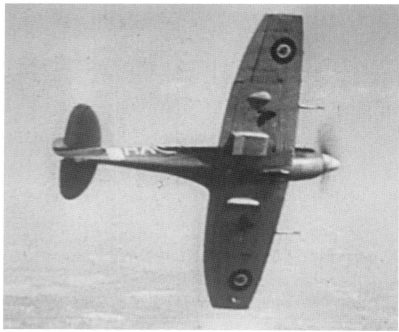

Above left: 179. The nature of the air war began changing in 1942. The previous year, RAF fighters had begun flying in support of the Army in North Africa. To make the Spitfire more manoeuvrable at low level, the wing-tips were removed, leading pilots to consider these aircraft 'clipped, cropped and clapped'! This is a clipped-wing Mk VB at 52 Operational Training Unit, Aston Down.

Left: 180. A clipped-wing Spitfire Mk VB in profile.

Above: 181. A Spitfire Mk VB in plan view.

Above: 182. Further evidence of Fighter Command's multinational composition: 19 Squadron's Free French pilot, Rene Royer, at Perranporth with his Spitfire Mk VB, EP445, in 1942. (Roger Henderson)

Above right: 183. By now Spitfire production at Castle Bromwich was in overdrive, churning out Spitfires.

Right: 184. In June 1942, Fighter Command at last received the Spitfire Mk IX – able to match the FW 190, and which turned the tide at last. This is Flight Lieutenant Bob Poulton of 64 Squadron at Kenley with one of those early machines. Note the four-bladed propeller, required by the engine's two-stage supercharger.

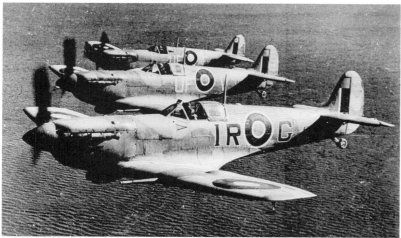

Above left: 185. In the Western Desert Spitfires were first used as fighter-bombers. This is an early Mk V in North Africa, armed with two 250-lb bombs.

Above: 186. The desert fighting dictated reinforcement by various home squadrons, including 72. Here Flight Lieutenant David Cox poses with his desert Mk V, also named after his wife. The living conditions were primitive, operating conditions testing.

Left: 187. Wing Commander Ian 'Widge' Gleed leading a section of Spitfires off Tunisia, his Wing Leader's pennant and personal initials clearly visible.

Above: 188. A clipped-wing Mk VB over the desert.

Above right: 189. A Desert Air Force Mk VB taxies for take-off from a Tunisian airfield. Such airstrips were improvised, evidenced by the steam-roller.

Right: 190. An excellent close-up of the Vokes Air Filter on a Desert Air Force Spitfire Mk VC.

Left: 191. A Spitfire Mk VC is turned around in its sand-bagged revetment. Note fuel being poured in by way of a tin can.

Above: 192. The Mediterranean island of Malta was heavily besieged by Axis forces and subjected to sustained heavy air attacks. Strategically the island was crucial to operations in that theatre, so had to be held at all costs. On 7 March 1942, fifteen Spitfires eventually reached the island. This is one of them, preparing to take off from HMS *Eagle*.

Opposite top left: 193. The menace from German high-altitude reconnaissance bombers had led to the development of the first high-altitude Spitfire variant, the Mk VI, but this was essentially a Mk V and was not really powerful enough. The Merlin 61 of the Mk IX, however, provided more opportunity, and so the Mk VII was born. With a service ceiling of 39,500 feet and a pressurised cockpit, this aircraft flew higher than ever before. Interestingly, while wings had been clipped for low-level operations, for high-altitude work the wing-tips of these Spitfires were extended – as indicated by this photograph. As the high-altitude threat passed, the Mk VII was phased out of production by 1944, 140 having been built.

Above: 194. Back in England, Fighter Command's front-line squadrons were all now equipped with the Spitfire Mk IX – like this aircraft of the Polish 317 Squadron.

Right: 195. Many experienced RAF fighter pilots fought on Malta, including Battle of Britain veterans who described that 1940 contest as 'child's play' compared to the battles over the beleaguered Mediterranean island. This is Flight Lieutenant Johnny Plagis, a Rhodesian of Greek origin, and one of Malta's most successful aces. After remaining in the post-war RAF, Plagis returned to Rhodesia where he committed suicide. Pilots like Plagis, though, won the air battle for Malta, writing another chapter in the Spitfire 'Legend'.

5

THE TURNING TIDE: 1943

By now, P-51 Mustangs, with a range of 2,200 miles, were fulfilling a dedicated escort role from English airfields, as the American daylight bomber offensive continued, slowly relieving the Spitfire of this role. As ever, the war's progress dictated Spitfire deployment. The years 1941 and 1942 had been disastrous for the Allies in the Far East, culminating in the fall of Singapore on 15 February 1942. With a full-scale British retreat from Burma underway, it seemed that the Japanese were unstoppable in tropical climes. Japan's control of New Guinea put the Australian mainland within range of their bombers. Three squadrons of Spitfires, however, were based near Darwin: on 2 May, thirty-three Spitfire Mk Vs successfully engaged the first major Japanese raid on Darwin. The Spitfire was faster than the Japanese Mitsubushi Zero fighter, and the light enemy machine was vulnerable to cannon fire. With the Americans sending an increasing amount of troops to the Pacific Theatre, beginning their 'Island Hopping' campaign, pressure began mounting on the so far victorious Japanese.

On 10 July 1943 Spitfires supported the Allied invasion of Sicily. It was really from here on that the air war, and the Spitfire's role within it, began changing significantly. Also up over the Salerno beachhead were Supermarine Seafires, the carrier version of this most famous of fighters. The Allied fighters provided a protective umbrella to the troops below. The German *blitzkrieg* in the West during May 1940 had perfectly demonstrated the advantages of tactical co-operation between air and ground forces. The British had eventually worked out this technique in North Africa, and put these lessons to successful effect in Sicily. Now Spitfires operating in the Mediterranean theatre found themselves not so much dogfighting Luftwaffe fighters, but increasingly employed strafing and dive-bombing German troops. It was here, of course, that the foundations of Allied tactical air power were laid – and which, the following year, would prove decisive.

Over enemy-occupied Europe, the Spitfire's war continued largely unchanged. On 24 February 1943 the Spitfire Mk XII reached the RAF, heralding a new phase of Spitfire development. This machine looked very different from the early Merlin-engined variants, largely because it had a completely new Rolls-Royce Griffon engine, and was an interim expedient, pending arrival of the improved Mk XIV. Intended for low-altitude sorties, the Mk XII's top speed was 397 mph. By October, the Mk XIV was in service, with a maximum speed of 448 mph, a service ceiling of 45,500 feet. Impressive though these statistics were, the fact remained that the new Spitfire's range was only 850 miles.

Having undertaken major combined operations and harnessed tactical air power in Sicily and Italy, the Allies planned to launch the liberation of enemy-occupied Europe from British soil. To effect the necessary air operations in advance of and after the proposed landings, the 2nd Tactical Air Force (TAF) was created, which also benefited from the Desert Air Force's (DAF) experience. In August 1943, the fighter wings based at the various Sector Stations became known as 'Airfields'. These formations began practising a nomadic existence, living under canvas and being self-sufficient, able to move quickly and at short notice. This was ready for the days ahead when the advancing Allied armies would require rapid tactical air support. By now, the Luftwaffe was seriously under pressure, defending the Reich by day against American bombers and RAF Bomber Command's 'heavies' at night. Moreover, after the catastrophic German defeat at Stalingrad in February 1943, Stalin's forces were advancing ever westwards. In the Far East too, the tide had long since turned, and the Allies were advancing on all fronts – albeit at great cost. Clearly the time was fast approaching for a cataclysmic finale – in which the Spitfire would continue to play its part.

Above right: 196. The RAF training manual *Tee Em* featured the cartoon character 'Pilot Officer Prune' – represented here as a bad shot, firing not on the drogue but at the Lysander towing it!

Right: 197. Another Spitfire development was the tear-drop canopy, improving visibility, seen here on Spitfires on the Castle Bromwich assembly line. The foremost aircraft shows the cannon and ammunition drum, machine-gun bays, and clipped wing.

Above left: 198. Spitfire Mk IXs, together with Avro Lancasters, await production flight tests at Castle Bromwich in 1943.

Above right: 199. Spitfire Mk VBs outside Westland Aircraft.

Left: 200. Production testing at Castle Bromwich was in the hands of Alex Henshaw, a remarkable pre-war airman and a skilled exponent of the Spitfire. Alex is pictured centre, in white test pilot's overalls, with his team in 1943.

Above: 201. A pair of 611 Squadron Spitfire Mk IXs.

Right: 202. Throughout the war, the Spitfire continued to be used for propaganda purposes, and, above all others, became the icon associated with the British nation's struggle against overwhelming odds in the early war years. This advertisement, appearing in 1943 and emphasising the co-operation between the aircraft and automotive industries, demonstrated to great effect by Castle Bromwich, features the Spitfire Mk IX.

Above left: 203. Armourers re-arm a Spitfire Mk IX 'somewhere in England'.

Left: 204. Flying Officer Robert Martin Davidson, of 222 Squadron at Hornchurch, with Spitfire Mk IX MA509 'Uruguay XVI'. This aircraft also flew with 152 Squadron in North Africa and provided cover for the Anzio beachhead with 94 Squadron in 1944. Sadly Davidson was killed in action, on 6 April 1945, flying a Hawker Tempest Mk V. (Peter Davidson via Steve Bown)

Above right: 205. Home-based fighter squadrons were now employed constantly on cross-Channel operations, either sweeps over France or escorting American daylight bombers. Although always hampered by a lack of range, the tide was turning in the Spitfire pilots' favour. This is 19 Squadron's Flight Lieutenant Tommy Drinkwater, who destroyed the unit's 100th enemy aircraft on 11 November 1943. As the Spitfire Mk IX pictured displays a squadron leader's rank pennant, it presumably belongs to the CO, Squadron Leader Vic Ekins. Note also the round-style exterior rear-view mirror, common on all Spitfires from the Mk IX onwards.

Above: 206. The most successful Spitfire of all was Mk IX EN398, the personal mount of Wing Commander Johnnie Johnson, leader of the Canadian Wing at Kenley in 1943. Johnson, pictured here with that aircraft, which sports both his initials and the maple leaf insignia, destroyed twelve of his final score of thirty-eight and a half enemy aircraft destroyed, five shared and five more damaged.

Above right: 207. The Spitfire Mk VII continued in service, although largely employed on normal operations. These aircraft had been painted light grey for high-altitude work, in which scheme they remained. This photograph shows clearly the pressurised cockpit, pointed rudder and wing-tips.

Right: 208. Wing Commander Johnnie Johnson aloft from Kenley in a factory-fresh Spitfire Mk IX in 1943.

Above left: 209. Maison Blanch in Algiers became a staging point for allied aircraft pending the invasion of Sicily. This is a Spitfire Mk VC of 152 Squadron seen there soon before the invasion – note the temporary runway surface. (Rob Rooker)

Above: 210. On 10 July 1943, the Allies invaded Sicily, from which Mediterranean island the invasion of Italy was launched the following year. Here personnel of 152 Squadron receive a briefing concerning the dangers of malaria on Sicily. The Spitfire Mk VC sports the Desert Air Force's yellow cross motif on the engine cowling. (Rob Rooker)

Left: 211. These are Spitfire Mk IXs of 152 Squadron, operating from a dusty airstrip while supporting those campaigns. Increasingly, Spitfire pilots found themselves not mixing it with enemy fighters but engaged on ground-attack sorties.

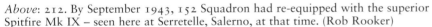

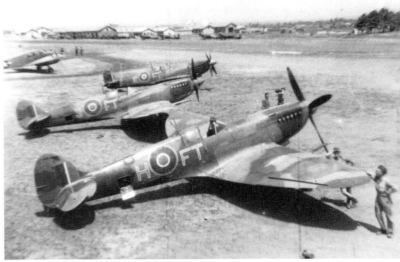

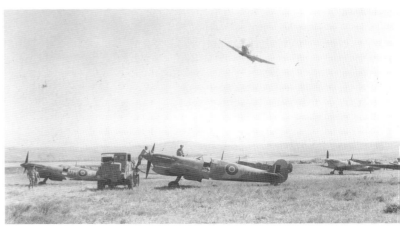

Above: 212. By September 1943, 152 Squadron had re-equipped with the superior Spitfire Mk IX – seen here at Serretelle, Salerno, at that time. (Rob Rooker)

Above right: 213. Spitfire Mk IXs of 43 Squadron at Catania, Sicily, 1943. The centre aircraft was that of a flight commander, Flight Lieutenant Ron Rayner. The foremost aircraft shows an open hatch, providing access to flying control wires. Codes of these aircraft were red, outlined in white.

Right: 214. A Spitfire Mk VC of 152 Squadron over-flies other squadron aircraft at Lentini East, on the Italian mainland in July 1943. (Rob Rooker)

6

LIBERATION & TOTAL VICTORY: 1944–1945

Throughout 1943 and 1944, American military personnel and materiel had stockpiled in England, ready for the long-awaited Second Front. Such a huge combined operation was unprecedented. The plan called for Allied airborne troops to drop in advance of seaborne landings and capture key objectives. Allied bombers would soften up coastal defences, which would then be pounded by a devastating naval barrage. Then, British, Canadian and American troops would storm the Normandy beaches. The Allied invasion – D-Day – was launched on 6 June 1944. A huge screen of fighters ensured that the Luftwaffe failed to hinder the landings. Before and after D-Day, however, Spitfires were increasingly employed as fighter-bombers, harassing and destroying the enemy wherever he could be found. So complete, in fact, was Allied air superiority over the Normandy battlefield that the Germans were only able to move troops under cover of darkness. Soon Spitfires were operating from French soil, extending their range of penetration over enemy territory, the 2nd TAF pilots becoming well versed in dive-bombing and ground-attack. By mid-August the Germans had no choice but to retreat across the River Seine via what became known as the 'Falaise Gap'. There the Allied fighter-bombers pounded the enemy – German casualties are estimated at some 300,000; only 20,000 German soldiers safely crossed the Seine. The following month, the ambitious but ill-fated Operation MARKET GARDEN was launched by Allied airborne forces to capture bridges across the Rhine in Holland. Unlike Normandy, however, the confused and close-quarters nature of the fighting prevented any major support being provided by Allied fighter-bombers. Ultimately the operation, intended to end the war by Christmas, failed and the Allies continued their long, bloody, slog to cross the Rhine and fight their way across Germany.

Of course, as the Spitfire's performance had increased over the years, so had that of the two main German fighters, the Me 109 and FW 190. During mid-1944, however, a new German fighter was committed to battle – the jet-powered Me 262. With a top speed of 559 mph, the 262's debut heralded the end of all piston-engined fighters. The 262 represented the first of a whole new generation of aircraft, the performance of which was incomparable to the existing types in service. Nonetheless, on 5 October 1944 the Spitfires of 401 Squadron caught and destroyed the first enemy jet to be despatched: invincible the 262 may not have been, but its superior performance and the jet engine's potential for future development was clear to all. Not the 262 or Hitler's rocket bombs, the V-1 and V-2, could turn the tide of war, which had long been lost for Nazi Germany. With Allied and Soviet troops having linked up on the Elbe, as the Battle for Berlin raged in the doomed city, and the Reich lay in ruins all around, Hitler committed suicide on 30 April 1945. On 8 May 1945, Germany surrendered unconditionally, concluding the war in Europe.

The war in the Fast East, however, had yet to end. Hurricanes had equipped the RAF air component operating in that theatre, until the arrival of Spitfires and P-51s in 1944. In spite of the long-term sea blockade and fire-bombing of Japanese cities, this Far Eastern adversary continued to fight determinedly. By July 1945, the carriers of Task Force 37 were in the Pacific, just 30 miles from Tokyo. Terminally weakened by the blockade, however, Japan surrendered unconditionally, on 15 August 1945, after the second of two atomic bombs was dropped by the Americans. The Second World War was at last over, and so too was the Spitfire's finest hour; or was it?

Left: 215. Re-organised into the 2nd Tactical Air Force, by 1944 the home-based Spitfire squadrons were already practising for the invasion of enemy-occupied France. This would entail tactical deployment, supporting the Army, flying from temporary airfields, able to move quickly and at short-notice. Squadrons moved to airfields in the South of England, living in tented accommodation and with mobile workshops. Here, Wing Commander Johnnie Johnson leads his Canadians off, in a clipped-wing Spitfire LF Mk IX, from Lashenden.

Below left: 216. A 222 Squadron pilot poses with his damaged Spitfire Mk IX in early 1944, captioned, 'Don't argue with the front-end of a 190' in Squadron Leader Bob Beardsley's album.

Below: 217. Another of Bob's photographs, showing a damaged 222 Squadron Mk IX, captioned, 'Its that flak again!'

Above: 218. Spitfire Mk IVX; note, again, the clipped wing for low-level work.

Above right: 219. A Spitfire Mk IVX complete with 'D-Day Stripes'.

Right: 220. This high-flying Spitfire Mk VIII was built in 1944.

Opposite: 221. A Griffon-engined Photographic Reconnaissance Spitfire, fitted with oblique cameras.

Above: 222. Soon, Spitfires were operating from Norman cornfields.

Above right: 223. Spitfires being serviced in the field, during the Normandy Campaign.

Right: 224. D-Day striped Spitfires of 222 Squadron at Merville, France.

Above left: 225. An unknown Australian pilot of 222 Squadron with his Spitfire Mk IX at Merville. Unusually, the Squadron's Spitfires had no stripes on their wings. In the cockpit, the new gyro gun sight can be seen.

Above: 226. Another unknown 222 Squadron pilot in France, a close-up showing off the Mk IX's nose in detail.

Left: 227. Flight Lieutenant Kazek Budzik of 308 (Polish) Squadron with his bombed-up Spitfire Mk IX on 29 October 1944. Minutes later, Budzik strafed an enemy staff car but was shot down by flak near the Dutch Breda–Dordrecht Bridge. He crash-landed and was back in action almost immediately.

Opposite: 228. Over Normandy, the Allied fighter-bombers ruled the skies. This is Wing Commander Geoffrey Page, a Wing Leader, setting off for another 'Armed Reconnaissance' over Normandy.

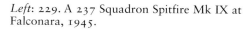

Left: 229. A 237 Squadron Spitfire Mk IX at Falconara, 1945.

Below left: 230. Flight Lieutenant John Slade's 237 Squadron Spitfire Mk IX in Italy, 1945.

Below: 231. In 1945, the war still raged in Italy, where flak was also a constant threat to Spitfire pilots engaged in ground-attack. This is Flight Lieutenant Ron Rayner's 72 Squadron ground crew at Ravenna with his flak-damaged Mk IX.

Above: 232. Back in England: a wrecked 1 Squadron Spitfire Mk IX at Manston, March 1945.

Above right: 233. Spitfires also flew Photographic Reconnaissance sorties over Japanese territory. This is a Spitfire PR XI, clearly showing the enlarged air intake required for the two-stage Merlin, and a 'slipper' auxiliary fuel tank. The aircraft is airborne over India in 1945.

Right: 234. The Griffon-engined mount of Wing Commander Johnnie Johnson, pictured in Germany, 1945. This engine required a five-bladed propeller.

Above left: 235. This is former Battle of Britain Hurricane pilot Squadron Leader Laurence 'Rubber' Thorogood, CO of 273 Squadron, on Ramree Island, in April 1945. The squadron leader's rank pennant is shown in detail.

Above: 236. Warrant Officer Jimmy Chuck (right) and ground crew of 152 Squadron at Tamu, Burma, in 1944. (Rob Rooker)

Left: 237. Home in England, at Hamble, near Southampton, wrecked Spitfire Mk IXs, all with D-Day markings and mostly from Canadian squadrons, are unceremoniously scrapped.

Above right & above: 238 & 239. The Spitfire's future: Alex Henshaw testing the prototype Griffon-engined Mk 22. Ultimately there were twenty-four marks of Spitfire, this machine representing the last development stage.

Right: 240. Although replaced by jets as a front-line fighter after the war, the Spitfire still saw action in various roles and theatres, not least in Malaya. This aircraft, a PR IXX, PS853, made the last operational Spitfire flight on 9 June 1957, a weather data-recording flight for the Temperature & Humidity Testing Flight based at Woodvale in Lancashire. It was then allocated to the RAF Memorial Flight at Coltishall, and now still flies with the RAF's Battle of Britain Memorial Flight based at Coningsby in Lincolnshire.

CONCLUSION

The Supermarine Spitfire entered the Second World War as the RAF's best front-line fighter. By 1945, the RAF had one squadron equipped with a jet fighter, the Gloster Meteor, which was the shape of things to come. The Spitfire, however, was still the RAF's best piston-engined fighter. That said, the Spitfire had gone through so many modifications and improvements that the Griffon-engined growlers of 1944 onwards bore little resemblance to the little prototype that first alighted from Eastleigh in 1936. The Spitfire was originally envisaged and designed as a short-range defensive interceptor, a role in which it excelled. From 1941 onwards Mitchell's fighter had been pressed into service as a long-range offensive and escort fighter, high-altitude interceptor and photographic reconnaissance machine, low-level fighter-bomber and, known as the Seafire, even operated from aircraft carriers. All of this provides ample evidence of the flexibility and long-term potential of Mitchell's design, especially when compared to the Hawker Hurricane. That the Spitfire was ahead of its time in 1936 is indisputable. After the Second World War, the Spitfire's fighting days were not, in fact, over. Spitfires saw active service in the subsequent Malayan Emergency, and, having been sold to both the Egyptian and Israeli air forces, Spitfire even fought Spitfire over the Middle East. Finally, in 1957, the Spitfire made its last operational flight with the RAF before becoming a museum piece in a world dominated by jet aircraft.

The Spitfire's contribution to the Allied war effort, however, was not just limited to the world's aerial battlegrounds. The Spitfire gripped the public imagination in a way no other aircraft has ever achieved before or since. In 1940, for example, so-called 'Spitfire Funds' swept the free world, patriotic citizens raising cash for Spitfires – although very small numbers of other aircraft types were 'presented' to the government in this way, the public's preference for and preoccupation with the Spitfire was apparent from this phenomenon. Before and during the war, of course, it was necessary to generate confidence in the Spitfire for the public to believe that here was the wonder weapon that would save Britain from the dreaded German bombers. Consequently a myth was soon woven around the Spitfire, one which has since been maintained and reworked over time. Today the Spitfire has evolved into a symbol of British national pride and superiority, harking back to the glory days of Empire and victory in the Second World War. An increasing number of Spitfires, it seems, are restored to airworthiness annually, delighting air show crowds. Indeed, the Spitfire truly remains alive and well in British popular culture.

In conclusion, one thing is certain: there has never been another aircraft as uniquely inspirational as the Spitfire, partly because the Spitfire story is inexorably connected with that of 1940 – the one year that encapsulates everything about former British greatness. Hopefully Spitfires will continue to grace our infinitely more peaceful skies for many years to come. What, I wonder, would R. J. Mitchell think, to know not only how much his Spitfire contributed to victory in the Second World War, but equally that, over seventy years after it first flew, the story of his little fighter is still far from over?

BIBLIOGRAPHY

Bader, D. R. S., *Fight for the Sky: The Story of the Spitfire & Hurricane* (1st edn, London: Sidgwick & Jackson, 1973).

Boot, H., and R. Sturtivant, *Gifts of War: Spitfires and Other Presentation Aircraft in Two World Wars* (1st edn, Tonbridge: Air-Britain, 2005).

Mitchell, G., *R. J. Mitchell, World Famous Aircraft Designer: From Schooldays to Spitfire* (1st edn, Olney: Nelson & Saunders, 1986).

Morgan, E., and E. Shacklady, *Spitfire: The History* (1st edn, Stamford: Key Publishing, 1987).

Price, A., *The Spitfire Story* (2nd edn, London: Arms & Armour, 1995).

Ramsey, W. (ed.), *The Battle of Britain: Then & Now, Mk V* (London: After the Battle, 1989).

Sarkar, D., *Bader's Tangmere Spitfires: The Untold Story, 1941* (1st edn, Sparkford: PSL, 1996).

Sarkar, D., *Bader's Duxford Fighters: The Big Wing Controversy* (1st edn, Worcester: Ramrod Publications, 1997).

Sarkar, D., *The Few: The Battle of Britain in the Words of the Pilots* (1st edn, Stroud: Amberley Publishing, 2009).

Sarkar, D., *Spitfire Voices: Life as a Spitfire Pilot in the Words of the Veterans* (1st edn, Stroud: Amberley Publishing, 2010).

Sarkar, D., *The Spitfire Manual 1940* (1st edn, Stroud: Amberley Publishing, 2010).

Sarkar, D., *How the Spitfire Won the Battle of Britain* (1st edn, Stroud: Amberley Publishing, 2010).

Websites

http://www.dilipsarkarmbe.co.uk: Dilip Sarkar's personal site.

http://www.152hyderabad.co.uk: Rob Rooker's excellent site dedicated to 152 Squadron.

http://www.spitfiresociety.com: The Spitfire Society.

http://www.raf.mod.uk/bbmf: The RAF Battle of Britain Memorial Flight.

OTHER BOOKS BY DILIP SARKAR

Spitfire Squadron: No 19 Squadron at War, 1939-41

The Invisible Thread: A Spitfire's Tale

Through Peril to the Stars: RAF Fighter Pilots Who Failed to Return, 1939-45

Angriff Westland: Three Battle of Britain Air Raids Through the Looking Glass

A Few of the Many: Air War 1939-45, A Kaleidoscope of Memories

Bader's Tangmere Spitfires: The Untold Story, 1941

Bader's Duxford Fighters: The Big Wing Controversy

Missing in Action: Resting in Peace?

Guards VC: Blitzkrieg 1940

Battle of Britain: The Photographic Kaleidoscope, Volume I

Battle of Britain: The Photographic Kaleidoscope, Volume II

Battle of Britain: The Photographic Kaleidoscope, Volume III

Battle of Britain: The Photographic Kaleidoscope, Volume IV

Fighter Pilot: The Photographic Kaleidoscope

Group Captain Sir Douglas Bader: An Inspiration in Photographs

Johnnie Johnson: Spitfire Top Gun, Part I

Johnnie Johnson: Spitfire Top Gun, Part II

Battle of Britain: Last Look Back

Spitfire! Courage & Sacrifice

Spitfire Voices: Life as a Spitfire Pilot in the Words of the Veterans

The Battle of Powick Bridge: Ambush a Fore-thought

Duxford 1940: A Battle of Britain Base at War

Hearts of Oak: The Human Tragedy of HMS Royal Oak

The Few: The Battle of Britain in the Words of the Pilots

The Last of the Few: Eighteen Battle of Britain Pilots Tell Their Extraordinary Stories

How the Spitfire Won the Battle of Britain

The Spitfire Manual

Spitfire Ace of Aces: The True Wartime Story of Johnnie Johnson Douglas Bader

As Editor: *Spitfire! The Experiences of a Battle of Britain Fighter Pilot*, by Brian Lane.

As contributor: *Battle of Britain: The Movie*, by Robert Rudhall.

Also available from Amberley Publishing

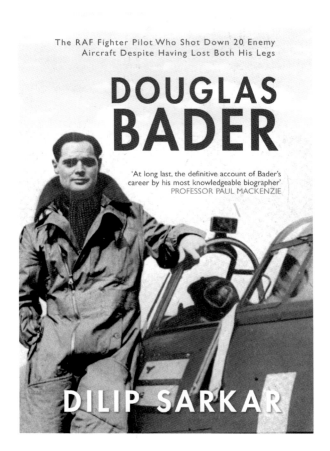

The RAF Fighter Pilot Who Shot Down 20 Enemy
Aircraft Despite Having Lost Both His Legs

DOUGLAS
BADER

'At long last, the definitive account of Bader's
career by his most knowledgeable biographer'
PROFESSOR PAUL MACKENZIE

DILIP SARKAR

Also available from Amberley Publishing

How to fly the legendary fighter plane in combat using the manuals and instructions supplied by the RAF during the Second World War

'A Must' *INTERCOM: THE AIRCREW ASSOCIATION*

An amazing array of leaflets, books and manuals were issued by the War Office during the Second World War to aid pilots in flying the Supermarine Spitfire, here for the first time they are collated into a single book with the original 1940s setting. An introduction is supplied by expert aviation historian Dilip Sarkar. Other sections include aircraft recognition, how to act as an RAF officer, bailing out etc.

£9.99 Paperback
40 illustrations
264 pages
978-1-84868-436-2

Also available as an ebook
Available from all good bookshops or to order direct
Please call **01453-847-800**
www.amberleybooks.com

Also available from Amberley Publishing

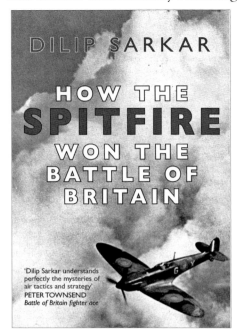

Finally lays to rest the myth that the Hurricane won the Battle of Britain rather than the numerically inferior, yet more glamorous, Spitfire

'Dilip Sarkar understands perfectly the mysteries of air tactics and strategy'
PETER TOWNSEND, *Battle of Britain fighter ace*

Featuring interviews with pilots who flew to war in both Spitfires and Hurricanes, and following a detailed analysis of combat reports and casualty records, Dilip Sarkar shatters the myth that the Hawker Hurricane won the Battle of Britain.

£18.99 Hardback
40 Photographs
160 pages
978-1-84868-868-1

Also available as an ebook
Available from all good bookshops or to order direct
Please call **01453-847-800**
www.amberleybooks.com

Also available from Amberley Publishing

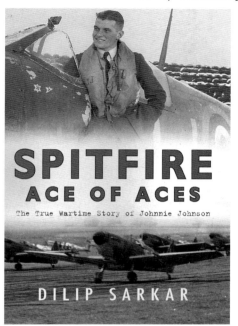

The biography of the RAF's top fighter pilot, Johnnie Johnson who shot down more enemy aircraft than any other pilot during the Second World War

Johnnie Johnson is a character literally straight out of the pages of 'Boys Own'. By the end of the Second World War the RAF Spitfire pilot was a household name in Britain, feted by Churchill and Eisenhower. Although he missed the Battle of Britain when slow flying bombers were abundant and easy targets for fighters by 1945 he had notched up 38 ¹/₂ enemy 'kills' – all fighters which took far more skill to shoot down - and officially the RAF's top-scoring fighter ace.

£25 Hardback
127 Photographs
320 pages
978-1-4456-0475-6

Also available as an ebook
Available from all good bookshops or to order direct
Please call **01453-847-800**
www.amberleybooks.com

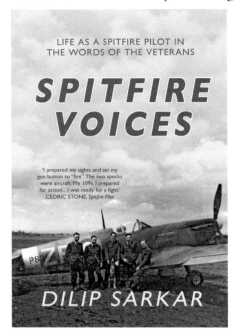